CHRISTOPHER J. STOCKWELL

City Attorney's Office

Book One: Professional Camouflage

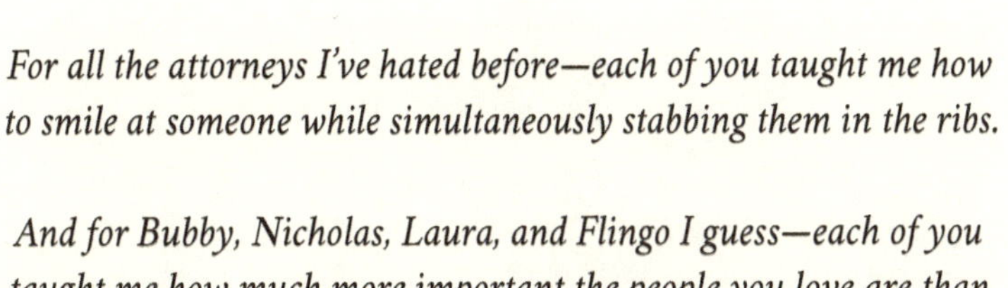

For all the attorneys I've hated before—each of you taught me how to smile at someone while simultaneously stabbing them in the ribs.

And for Bubby, Nicholas, Laura, and Flingo I guess—each of you taught me how much more important the people you love are than the people you hate.

Once you get people laughing, they're
listening and you can tell them almost
anything.

—HERBERT GARDNER

Preface

"Why do you write?" She asked me.

"Because none of this makes any sense to me anymore" is what Ben would say.

Humans beings can conjure bogeymen from anything. We materialize polarization everywhere, even within our own ideological tents. If you're left, I'm further left. If you right, I'm further right. Crises often bring people of different (but similar) ideological banners together, but those alliances are temporary, and quickly discarded in favor of more intra-ideological battles. Conflict is human homeostasis, and there's no fix for our short-sighted adversarial nature. These ideological tents can be as large as a confederacy composed of disagreeing nations and as small as one person with a beef against their roommate.

I'm a lawyer, a former prosecutor. Our profession is adversarial in nature. It's also toxic, and not an occupation fit for humans beings, at least not decent well-meaning ones. A courtroom is an arena, a lawyer is a gladiator, and words are swords. Is there room for cooperation, fellowship, and love in such a world? Probably not, but maybe.

Why do I write, because even though there's no solution to the problem of being human, I still want to tell you what I think about it.

Acknowledgement

I would like to acknowledge and give my warmest thanks to the line prosecutors I served with at the Criminal Division of the Seattle City Attorney's Office. Crackin' jokes and complainin' about that place with all of you will always be some of my favorite memories.

Chapter 1

H e'd fallen ass-backwards into that job, just as he fell ass-backwards into most things. It wasn't that he'd ended up there accidently. He'd done everything quite intentionally. It's just that he'd seen the job announcement on the last day that it was open. It was also that a new city attorney had just been elected in Seattle. Pete Holmes had been only marginally to the left of the city attorney he defeated in the 2009 election, but a marginal ideology difference in Seattle politics often turned out to be an uncrossable chasm for many a politician. Welcome to Seattle, the place where political careers go to die. That change in leadership had opened up an opportunity—that is, the city attorney's office had suffered a mass exodus in December 2009 and January 2010.

Many who had feared new leadership left of their own accord. Others had been casualties of the ritual ideological herd culling by the new administration. Either way, there had been an opportunity for someone like Ben to slide into a job as a prosecutor at the city attorney's office. "I was punching way above my weight class landing that job, but I showed up and hoped that nobody would figure out that I didn't belong. I'd started putting on that professional camouflage way back in middle school. I always got thrown into the advance classes, but unfortunately that meant that I went from being the smartest person in a class full of dum-dums to the dumbest person in a class full of smart-ass overachievers."

Ben had been getting by in this manner most of his life, and one day at the city attorney's office convinced him that he'd be able to continue his mediocre string of successes by hiding in plain sight. This was mostly accomplished by not talking too much. Ben was smart, but he was usually surrounded by people who were more intelligent than he was. What he'd noticed long ago, however, was that people, smart and dumb alike, tended to talk too much when they became flustered. Women did it, men did it, kids definitely did it. "You can catch a kid red-handed, covered in red paint, standing next to the dog he just painted red, and he'll tell you that Sally did it. Plus, he won't stop at telling you Sally did it. He'll come up with a whole narrative about how he was in the house watching TV when he heard the dog growling, and how he came out to investigate. If you confront him about being covered in paint, he'll give you some other nervously constructed long-winded explanation that exculpates him from the crime."

Ben knew that lies should be simple, straightforward, and believable. That's common sense to any storyteller. An assertively told lie projects confidence and therefore credibility. A narrow scope and simple fact pattern provide as yet unused arterials from which to amend a story as needed to accommodate future circumstances. Anyway, the best lie is the one that stays loaded in the cylinder, dormant, never seeing the light of day. That lie stays pristine. As soon as you pull the trigger and fire it into the world, it picks up tarnish. No matter how masterfully it's crafted, that dreaded patina begins to form once it exits your brain and enters the world.

Staying quiet, on the other hand, never degraded cautious pretenders such as Ben. In fact, staying quiet made one appear wise. Looking engaged made one appear judicious. Physical posturing made one appear both calm and confident. When speaking became unavoidable, repackaging what was just said by another tended to work pretty well. "But that's the survey-level class; I got a whole fuckin' graduate-level course on surviving a professional jungle with limited talent."

You couldn't even say that most of what was said that first week at the city attorney's office went in one ear and out the other because that would have required Ben to have actually registered what had been said on some level. No, most of it went right over his head. The general criminal law course is the first class that every law school student takes. For the majority of law school students, it's also the last criminal law course they will ever take. Most law students take their first-year classes and then spend years two and three focusing on the practice areas they are actually interested in. For most, that's civil law courses.

Ben was no different. He passed his first-year criminal law course and didn't give the subject another thought until he was studying for the bar. Passing the bar required revisiting long-forgotten subjects like criminal law. That was it, no other criminal-focused coursework or internships, nothing. Most of the people at the city attorney's office had spent the entirety of their time in law school learning criminal law, doing summer internships at prosecutor's offices, and generally preparing for careers as prosecutors. Ben passed the bar, sent out a few résumés to downtown law firms, and gave up on finding work as an attorney altogether. It was safe to say that Ben was cut from lazier cloth than his University of Washington Law School peers.

Two years after getting a license to practice law, Ben was working as a night-shift stocker at the QFC inside Broadway Market. One day, he saw a job announcement pop up on his LinkedIn page for Assistant City Prosecutors. Ben had actually been wondering why he even had a LinkedIn page when he saw the announcement. The more on-point observation would have been why he bothered checking it every day, since he never applied for any of the jobs he saw.

On both of the job interviews he'd had at downtown law firms, back when he was still sending out résumés, he'd blown it. They were entry-level jobs, and they were looking for fresh law school grads who had done coursework and internships in employment and labor law. He was specifically qualified for both positions, but something about being qualified for a position, and prepared for an interview, seized up his personality. He was wooden. He couldn't convey information in an interesting fashion. He was like the kid at the school assembly, trembling hands clutching his prepared speech, reading it verbatim without looking up even once to acknowledge the bleachers full of students.

Applying for the Assistant City Prosecutor job was a goof.

He didn't take it seriously. He knew he wasn't qualified and didn't expect to get an interview. He knew people from law school who had done internships at prosecutors' offices. They'd graduated magna cum laude, and they still hadn't gotten the job at the city attorney's office. But that was 2008, and the city attorney's office was a very different place in 2010. When he saw the announcement, he didn't realize the city attorney's office was in flux. He didn't realize they were desperate for warm bodies. He didn't realize they would hire anyone with a license to practice law that would take the job. He did get an interview, and since he had no expectation about actually getting the job, he crushed it.

He did make an effort. He did show up as well as he could. It's just that when someone acknowledges and accepts inevitable defeat, their true abilities rise to the surface. At least, that's how it worked for Ben. Fighters shout at you to "leave it all on the mat"; runners say to "let it all hang out"; baseball players tell you to "swing for the fences." But simple is better, and skateboarders just say "gnarly" anytime someone accomplishes something that is apparently undoable on a skateboard. Simple is better, but they all say the same thing: a person excels best when they have nothing left to lose.

On the day of the interview, Ben ironed the better of his two suits, the navy blue one. The gray one had peaked lapels, and the fabric was flat, not textured like the navy blue one. In fact, at that time Ben had two of almost everything: two suits, two white shirts, two ties. There was two of everything needed to get a job as a lawyer, everything except shoes. Ben had one pair of dress shoes. They were pretty nice, a mid-to-high-end brand sold at Nordstrom. He couldn't remember the brand, and the gold-embossed company markings on the inside heel of the shoes had long since worn off, but they were more than good enough for his purposes.

It was a panel interview, but not his first—the two interviews he'd had back in 2008 were panel interviews as well. Both of those were three-person panels with a very similar composition: a managing partner who sat silently, clearly uninterested in the entire affair; a token minority or woman to explain the firm's, air quotes, "commitment to diversity"; and a whip cracker—a mean middle-aged white guy who was the junior partner in charge of humiliating and torturing new associates.

The city attorney's panel was different. There were seven people: the Trial Unit supervisor, a domestic violence victim's advocate, the new Criminal Division Chief, the new elected City Attorney, the new City Attorney's Chief of Staff, the office manager, and lastly Maria Deloera. Maria was a line prosecutor from the Domestic Violence Unit. She was someone to Ben; he couldn't quite place who, but she was someone to him.

It wasn't just that there were a lot of interviewers, but it was a hot panel too. They kept throwing questions at Ben, sometimes lumping them on before he'd had an opportunity to answer the one asked just prior. At that interview, he appeared unflappable. Even when he didn't have a great answer, he brushed it off and kept rolling. Two weeks later, he got a call from the Trial Unit supervisor. A few days after that, an offer letter arrived in his mailbox.

Chapter 2

Ben was twelve when his brother died in 1993. Ben had just mastered the kickflip on his new Rodney Mullen deck. He was obsessed with Plan B's *Questionable* video. Rodney Mullen seemed like an alien super soldier in that video. The tricks he pulled off during his sequence were feats beyond human ability. They were, in a word, gnarly. It was appropriate that the first kickflip that Ben ever landed was on a deck bearing the name of the inventor of the kickflip.

The last time he had seen his brother was when he had come over for Sunday dinner a few weeks before. Ben had barely been able to ollie properly at that time, but Mike had grabbed Ben's board and ollied onto a bench at the church down the street from their house. He had done a 180 kickflip off the bench. It had been the best thing Ben had ever seen a skater do in real life. Mike was no Rodney Mullen, but he was good, and if he had focused on skating, he probably could have been great.

Mike hadn't been focused on skating for quite a while at the time of his death. Ben was vaguely aware of crack, and his parents didn't shield him from their conversations about Mike's problem. Ben knew it was a drug. He didn't know how destructive it was, but he knew it had hollowed out his brother—hollowed him out both emotionally and physically. The last time Ben saw him alive, at that Sunday dinner, he was a pale, gaunt caricature of himself. But not really a caricature. Caricatures exaggerate and poke fun in a good-natured way at someone's unique physical characteristics. A caricature of Mike at that point would have looked more like one of those Nazi Holocaust-era propaganda cartoons denoting Jews as dirty, sickly, and alien. There was nothing fun or light about Mike's appearance by that point. Mike's caricature could have been American government propaganda denoting the dangers of crack cocaine. And unlike the Nazi propaganda, the American propaganda would have been accurate.

It had only been a couple months before that when Ben had gotten the Rodney Mullen deck with the G-Bones wheels and Independent brand trucks. Mike and Ben's parents had given Mike $180 to get Ben a skateboard, his birthday present. They had also assumed there would be enough for lunch. There had been, but they hadn't gotten lunch that day.

Mike and Ben rode the bus over to Northwest Snowboards, and Mike had pointed toward the Rodney Mullen deck. He had pointed out the G-Bones wheels. He had strongly urged Ben to get the Independent brand trucks, not the Ventures. Ben actually preferred the Ventures later on, but at that time, Mike was his skate guru. To Ben it had seemed like a lot of money: forty-two dollars for a deck, thirty-five for wheels, forty for trucks, five for grip tape, and ten for bearings.

His parents had given him the new Airwalk Disaster shoes at the house before he and Mike left to go to the skate shop. His family wasn't rich, but his dad was a commercial electrician and a union member. Two hundred and change for a kid's birthday was a lot, but it certainly hadn't broken the budget.

After they left the skate shop, they'd gone over to Baker Middle School by their house. Mike had spent the rest of the afternoon showing Ben the fundamentals of street skating. "After that, Mike and I walked back to the house. He didn't come in. He didn't say goodbye to our parents. He gave me a hug, wished me a happy birthday, and strolled off toward the bus stop. He stuffed the receipt from the skate shop into my pocket in case I had to return something. When my parents asked me what we'd had for lunch and looked at the receipt from the skate shop, it wasn't hard for them to figure out why Mike took off without saying goodbye, and why there was no change. My mom made me a grilled-cheese sandwich. After that, she went upstairs and cried for a long time. My dad just sat in his chair flipping through channels, watching nothing in particular for most of the evening."

Ben never wanted to be like Mike. His crew—Mike, his best friend Jack, and his other friends Todd and Ron—had been societal miscreants, drunk and stoned juvenile delinquents who easily transitioned into hardened adult criminals and drug addicts. Ben loved and idolized his brother, but he also knew that he was severely fucked up. He had known his brother would die too soon. He had known it before everyone else had. Every hour he had spent with Mike that year he had spent like it was the last time he was going to see him, because he knew that one of those times in the not-too-distant future it would be the last time.

Ben knew that Mike actually had talents, and he had them in greater supply than Ben ever would. Despite great effort over many years on Ben's part, his strung-out malnourished brother had managed greater marvels on a skateboard that afternoon at Baker Middle School than Ben ever would. Unfortunately, the world had also saddled Mike with equal portions of vices that ensured he would flame out early. Ben had known he was powerless to change the trajectory of his brother's life, so he had loved him as best he could for as long as he was around.

Then he really was gone. Mike was shot less than three blocks from the four-story house of horrors that he lived in. "We went over to his place to clean it out after he died, but there was nothing to clean out." There was a stained mattress on the floor and a chair with so many black eyes and bruises it was hardly recognizable as a chair at all. The door was wide open when we got there, and the dead bolt was gone altogether.

That dead bolt hadn't gone far. Mike had been carrying it in a filthy sock when they found him. "Why did he go up to the Lucky 7 with a dead bolt in a sock? No one will ever know for sure, but I've had a lot of years to think about it. Since it was the last thing in his possession that might have had even the tiniest bit of value, he probably took it up there where the crack dealers were to see if he could get a rock for it. The other possibility is that he put it in the sock to use as a weapon to mug one of the crack dealers. Everyone knows a crack dealer shot him. Nobody knows which one. After all this time, I don't think it much matters to me who actually did it. It was going to happen that night or some other night. The person who shot him is likely dead as well by now."

Whoever it was likely never rose higher in life than dealing crack on a lonely street corner in a gritty little city. It seems like their punishment was implicit. "I just hate thinking about it. It hurts because it makes me not want to think about Mike at all, and so I find myself actively forgetting him a large part of the time now."

There was a man lying on the stained mattress when they got

there. There weren't even any clothes except for a Circle Jerks shirt that had burn marks and holes all over it. Ben took it. He still has it. It's in a box in his parents' attic. Since there was nothing else to salvage, Ben and his parents left that place. They didn't even bother to wake the writhing withdrawal-ridden form occupying the mattress.

Going into Mike's building was scary, but the three of them had been steeled by their righteous cause of reclaiming the possessions of their fallen loved one. Leaving, on the other hand, was a demoralizing retreat from a hostile landscape. Ben had seen his dad stick the .45 he kept on the high shelf in his bedroom closet into the back of his waistband before they left the house. He saw him load a magazine into the empty slot in the grip.

Ben's dad was Ben Sr., but after little Ben was born, people always referred to him as Big Ben. It made sense; he was big and tall, with muscles, a beard, and scraggly hair. His dad was a monolith in their neighborhood, like the actual Big Ben was a monolith on the London skyline. Big Ben presided over less impressive versions of himself up and down South Eighty-Third Street, from South Yakima Avenue all the way to South I Street. Big Ben saw little Ben as he was pulling his T-shirt down over the exposed handle of the 1911. It wasn't something his dad necessarily wanted little Ben to see him doing, so Big Ben just winked and gave him a thumbs-up. Little Ben returned the thumbs-up. He'd never seen his dad take that gun out of the closet. He only knew it was there because he'd been snooping in there a year or two before. To Ben, there wasn't anything his dad couldn't handle, so Ben gave it no more thought.

"Right then, leaving that place, I caught a glimpse of my dad's face. It was as though the notion that he might actually have to use his gun to get his wife and only remaining child out of that place alive had just occurred to him." That swagger and cocksure attitude were gone. In that moment, Big Ben was the scared child whistling in the dark. "My dad was more scared than me and my mom. We so completely believed in my dad's ability to handle anything." It lasted only a minute or two, but in that short time, his mask had cracked. There was a person inside the brick tower. He cried when he lost a son, and the thought of losing another rattled his otherwise unshakable foundation.

Ben heard screams coming from the other side of the cinderblock walls, and he saw orphaned corners adopted by the hordes of homeless crackheads that used Mike's building as both a crack market and a flophouse. Then he smelled something odd. He looked around and saw someone smoking crack using tinfoil and a hollowed-out Bic pen. He figured it was the smell of the plastic pen melting. Years later, he realized that was just how crack smelled.

Seeing how scared his dad was at that moment scared Ben. They were from South Tacoma. The neighborhood was rough, and his dad was the mayor of their block, the guy with a skilled trade and a masculine build, not to be trifled with. A few months before Mike died, there had been these bikers staying at that one house on the block, the house everyone knew about.

Every block in a blue-collar neighborhood has that house. Little Ben hadn't slept more than a few hours in at least a week on account of the noise coming from that house. One night his dad got up and walked over to that house in his wife-beater and boxers, no shoes. He kicked over a very shiny Harley with a custom-painted gas tank. Three guys came out. One walked straight up to Big Ben. "They were all yelling, saying they were going to kick his ass, you know the sort of shit you expect to hear in a situation like that. Big Ben didn't say a word. When the biker closest to him leaned in to hurl more hollow threats, Big Ben drove himself forward and headbutted that biker across the bridge of his nose. That guy's face exploded, blood shooting every-fuckin'-where." Big Ben had made his point, but he never liked having to do things more than once.

Big Ben felt that an unreasonable level of retaliation was always a reasonable response to unprovoked provocation. The two bikers who had initially confronted Big Ben grabbed their bloody friend and retreated. Next, Big Ben gestured to the two guys who were on the porch, then he kicked over another motorcycle. After some more yelling and posturing by the guys on the porch, he kicked over the third one too. All of a sudden, the yelling stopped, and the block was so quiet you could hear the traffic on Eighty-Fourth Street. "Basically, if you started an argument with my dad, he felt justified in destroying you, your entire family, and everyone you ever knew. I think that's what they call a scorched-earth policy."

Someone called the police, and Big Ben got locked up that night, but no one ever saw those bikers again, and the renters at that house became as tame as beat dogs. "On our street, Big Ben was lauded as a working-class hero, but he was also someone who neighbors walked on eggshells around. What scares a person like that? The fact that he was scared that night at Mike's apartment building terrified me. How could we be in a situation that he might not be able to handle? There was a group of guys standing in front of the elevator doors, and I saw my dad actually reach into the back of his waistband. Right then, he saw the door to the stairwell and directed me and my mom to it."

Ben cried. He mourned. It hurt, but he'd made himself ready for it. His parents hadn't accepted that Mike was unsalvageable while he was alive, so they imploded when he died. Ben mostly raised himself after that. "Mike had shown me what not to do. My parents had shown me the wrong way to handle loss. I started looking forward. I started looking past my house, my upbringing, my family, and most importantly I started looking at Tacoma as a place to put in my rearview mirror as soon as I could manage it."

Chapter 3

Ben didn't pick up on much of what was going on those first couple of weeks on the job. What he did take notice of was Maria. She was his peer mentor. She was supposed to show him the more practical aspects of the job, things like how to locate case files, how to put together discovery disclosures for defense attorneys, and so on. Mostly, what she did was bring Ben up to speed on all the current office gossip. While Ben was certainly interested in the shenanigans of the people who worked there, it wasn't helping him get his arms around the job itself. Maria herself was a somewhat significant distraction already. Other than that first-day gossip session, Ben didn't see much of Maria, and he began to think she didn't take her role as his peer mentor very seriously. Ben was sure he knew her, but there was so much whizzing by him, he set it aside for the time being.

It was only Tuesday. Ben rolled out of bed to the sound of his alarm clock. He was twenty-nine. People thought he was twenty-one. He felt like he was fifty. Skateboarding had not been kind to his body. When he sat in one position for more than an hour, his lower back tightened up and he had spasms. His knees were shot. When he was working as a night stocker at QFC, his knees were so painful that when he got home in the morning, he would take the store-brand Ibuprofen bottle out of his medicine chest and turn it upside down over his mouth, like he was chugging a beer. He didn't even bother to count them. There was a certain feeling he got in his mouth when there were six or seven of them in there. That feeling was his only guidepost. He'd chase them with one of the two Rainier tall boys he always brought home from work. Once he had a shower, he'd drink the other Rainier with the fried chicken and jojos he got at the QFC deli. Most mornings, he was so beat he'd just pass out in his chair. Sometime around ten or eleven in the morning, he'd wake up with a violent urge to piss. After that is when he would typically migrate to his bed.

But that was then and this was Tuesday, and Ben was waking up to put on one of his now three suits to start his third week at the city attorney's office. Stocking shelves on busted knees was hard, but to Ben, this was harder. Every morning he'd wake up at six. That, in and of itself, was miraculous. Ben had never once in his entire life woken up excited about the day to come. Even when he was little, even on Christmas morning, he wanted to be left alone to sleep. While everyone opened presents, he'd sit on the couch and wonder how much more he'd have to endure before he could go upstairs and go back to sleep. It was all he ever wanted, but it was also something that had eluded him his entire life. He never felt rested. In reality, he was never actually fully asleep. He always needed more because he never got any sleep worth having in the first place.

He'd gotten his first paycheck the previous Friday, and he went down to Nordstrom after work that evening and bought a pretty nice off-the-rack suit, and a couple more shirts and ties. The alterations were done on Monday, and Ben was now able to add a third suit to the weekly rotation. For his first two weeks, he'd been doing the navy blue on Monday, Wednesday, and Friday. He was wearing the dark gray one on Tuesdays and Thursdays. It made the most sense to wear the navy blue three times a week. It was the de facto uniform of a prosecutor, really of all lawyers who went to court on a regular basis. It was easy to assume that he, or any of the other male prosecutors in the office, had several dark blue suits. If you changed up the tie, nobody was the wiser. Still, getting the new light gray one and a few new ties into the rotation that week would make Ben feel less self-conscious.

Tuesday morning hurt. It hurt more than Monday morning. He expected to be miserable on Monday. Tuesday just felt like an extension of Monday, and the weekend seemed no closer to Ben than it had the day prior. He showered. He brushed his teeth. He parted his now clean-cut brown hair on the left side.

Getting dressed took at least ten minutes. He hadn't been wearing a suit long enough to be comfortable in one. The new light gray one was stiffer than the other two, and he constantly felt like the ass was going to tear open anytime he had to bend over for any reason. Tying his shoes hurt his knees. Tying his tie hurt his pride. Ben had fallen victim to the pattern that all men who had just started wearing a suit every day fell into. Every detail had to be perfect. He'd tie the tie four or five times to get the correct shape, size, and symmetry in the knot. He'd tuck and re-tuck his shirt constantly, trying to get the shirt to look flush with his pants. He'd push the belt buckle to the front of his pants. He'd pull his socks up over and over, trying to make the spandex-feeling fuckers hit the same point on each calf.

He was yet to realize that the tie knot was going to loosen

no matter how well he tied it, and the shirt was going to come largely untucked the second he sat down in his car. Everyone figures out how to get comfortable in uncomfortable constrictions given enough time. Also, nobody was even paying attention to the details. All anyone saw was some white guy with a dorky haircut in a boring-ass suit. "One day I did figure it out, and that day I added another arrow to my quiver full of professional camouflage arrows."

Seattle Municipal Tower—"SMT is what we called it"—was a huge biracial penis penetrating the Seattle skyline. It was clearly biracial because it was too dark to be a white guy, too light to be a Black guy. Maybe it could be Middle Eastern, Latino, Asian, who knows. Maybe it was a testament to Seattle's newfound commitment to racial diversity in the city's ruling white patriarchy. Unfortunately for the ladies, there were no gigantic vaginas of any skin tone in the city until the new football stadium was completed in 2002. That day the city gained a gigantic vagina. Unfortunately, they demolished the Kingdome to build it, so in gaining a vagina, the city also simultaneously lost a gigantic boob. Sorry ladies. Anyway, whatever SMT wasn't, it was clearly a huge penis. If it had been shaped any more like a penis, they would have had to dip it in gold and hide it in the background of *The Little Mermaid*'s movie poster. That little stunt was a beautiful little act of resistance by an underappreciated white-collar guerilla terrorist. Needless to say, any skyline, Seattle included, was choked with phalluses, but SMT was a throbbing cock among less ambitious phallic pretenders.

The Criminal Division of the Seattle City Attorney's Office was on the fifty-third floor of SMT, somewhere on the shaft slightly below the head, but well above the balls. Every morning as Ben and an elevator full of random city employees shot skyward in their little steel sperm, he felt as though they were traveling up SMT's main vein, about to be ejaculated out to impregnate the city sky. That exciting proposition was always smashed when Ben heard the telltale ding of the elevator arriving on fifty-three.

His key card—proof actual, as well as symbolic, that he was a preapproved member of this tribe—hung on a lanyard around his neck. He had been anointed as such by the chief of their tribe. "That shit cracked me up. It was fuckin' funny because that place really was like a tribe, and my boss was actually a chief—Criminal Division Chief. That was his actual job title. Plus, the city's logo is Chief Seattle. It was hard not to see the parallels everywhere. Walking into the office on any morning meant going to war with our rival tribe, the Department of Public Defense. The DPD was actually more like a coalition of several tribes. They squabbled among themselves, but they had one thing in common: they wanted to shoot an arrow through the heart of anyone under Chief Seattle's flag.

Chapter 4

When Ben was eight, NBC replayed both the original *V* miniseries and *V: The Final Battle*, the follow-up miniseries. There was a TV show that came after, but the network killed it after one season. Ben was obsessed from the opening scene. Fascist aliens use aspirational rhetoric and hollow promises to gain control of every lever of power on the planet without firing a shot. V was an entertaining and clever tool to show young people how powerful propaganda and rhetoric can be.

It could almost be seen as a piece of informative propaganda designed to expose corrosive propaganda for the smoke screen it was. Perhaps it was a form of Hollywood-inspired counterpropaganda. How it ever got green-lighted is a mystery to this day. Giving people a look behind the curtain at how vulnerable and thin human institutions really are was certainly not something the Reagan administration would have wanted. Exposing the bag of tricks that every propagandist has used since the first caveman stood on a tall rock and spoke from on high to the peons below is not anything anybody with fascist aspirations would ever want.

There were themes that were immediately clear to young Ben. Resist all forms of oppression, inequality, and domination.

Question everything you're told. Truth is an empirical process and the enemy of the powerful. He'd taken to carrying a can of red spray paint in his backpack that summer. He spray-painted his first "V" on the back of his house, in a place where there was a bush to cover his handiwork.

After that, he branched out to the Catholic church down the road, his school, the strip mall where the Korean lady's candy store was, the post office, and anywhere else there was a secluded wall. Little Ben knew, V doesn't stand for visitors. It stands for victory. "You understand? For victory. Go tell your friends." The words of the old Holocaust survivor from the miniseries, so powerful, ringing in young Ben's ears. He said it over and over again to anyone who would listen. When Big Ben found the "V" on the house, little Ben told his dad it was his birthright as a human being to resist all forms of oppression, inequality, and domination. Big Ben just laughed and told him their family was already part of the resistance and that he should go after the symbols of oppression. Little Ben assured Big Ben that he'd already gotten the church, strip mall, school, and post office.

Big Ben said, "Don't get caught, but if you do, I'll sort it out. Now get lost. I got to paint over this before your mother sees it and has a fit."

With that, Ben departed. He'd already gone full outlaw, but it was in the pursuit of justice. Outlaw yes, but he was a freedom fighter as well, saving humanity from itself, and possibly lizard aliens. Now he had the support of a higher authority. Ben's dad was camouflaged in plain sight. Union strong, malcontent, miscreant, he kept an aluminum baseball bat behind the bench seat of his Ford F-250 even though he never played baseball. If you knew the secret language, you could understand what he was really telling you. Ben understood. If you had the secret glasses, you could see what he saw, just like Rowdy Roddy Piper. If you tuned into the right pirate radio station, you could hear all of them broadcasting subtle defiance out on radio waves to an empty night sky.

From that day forward, Ben sought out the enemy like never before. He looked for those symbols of oppression, inequality, and domination everywhere, in every context. Practically every day, he rode his bike to the Fred Meyer on Seventy-Second Street. Nearly every day, he stole baseball cards, G.I. Joes, Star Wars action figures, and candy. And of course, Fred Meyer kept him well supplied with red spray paint.

These were the spoils of a campaign of resistance. At first, he kept his booty in his room, but hiding all those new toys became cumbersome. He started giving some of his stolen toys to other kids on the block. He had duplicates of dozens of figures, and he enjoyed stealing them more than he enjoyed playing with them, so he didn't mind just giving them away.

That summer, construction sites suffered as well. Late at night, Ben would sneak out of his house. There were houses being built two blocks over. Those construction sites had all sorts of useful things lying around. Carpenters would leave hammers, nails, even power tools. Everything that a kid might need to build a fort was sitting there for the taking. Ben took only what wouldn't be missed, or could easily be chalked up to misplacement. He got his first hammer there. A few nights later, he found a couple of screwdrivers. The next night, he took a box of nails. Every night after that for a couple of weeks, he hauled home one or two small scrapped two-by-fours or sheets of plywood. During the day, while his parents were at work, he'd build. Little by little a form took shape on the horizon. No one could say exactly what shape that form was, since Ben had never built anything, and he built unencumbered by the yolk of silly things like building plans and carpentry skills.

Ben's mother asked Big Ben multiple times where little Ben had acquired the building materials. He always told her that it was scrap material from his job sites. After a while, Big Ben started really looking at what little Ben was building, and after that, he actually did start bringing home scrap material from job sites. It was good timing, too, because the construction sites up the road had mostly finished with the building portion of the construction, and materials over there were becoming hard to come by.

Eventually, the fort in the backyard would span two rooms on the ground level and a crow's-nest type upper level. He'd built himself an outlaw's lair, or a resistance cell safe house. Maybe both. He wasn't really sure. He finally had a place to keep the piles of candy, action figures, and hundreds of other ill-gotten consumer goods he'd pilfered that year.

By the time he'd completed it, most of the summer had gone by, but he spent a solid two weeks sleeping in his fort. He took his meals out there and had a few epic sleepovers in the weeks before fourth grade started. That fort would stand for four years, before he deconstructed it the summer before he started eighth grade and built a half-pipe there. And of course, the front door of that fort, his nerve center, was adorned with a red "V" for victory.

Chapter 5

Maria was sitting in the driver's seat of her BMW in a haze of gray smoke. She had that Jawbreaker CD playing. The one that all the girls loved in 1995, *Dear You*. Guys loved *24 Hour Revenge Therapy*. It was seven in the morning, and getting baked in your car right on Level 2 of the SMT parking garage was probably not the wisest move. In prosecutorial terms, what she was doing was being in physical control of a vehicle while under the influence. It was a lesser included offense of driving under the influence, not that anybody was charging her. The Trial Unit prosecuted those, not the Domestic Violence Unit, where she worked. And as far as Maria was concerned, the DVU had a problem. His name was Alan Thorpe, her supervisor.

Alan Thorpe was a sleazy fucker by any metric, but the fact that he was the supervisor of the DVU made it even worse. The DVU's primary purpose and stated goal was to vindicate the interests of victims of domestic violence, almost exclusively women. Maria could tell by the way Alan interacted with the women in the office that he had no respect for them whatsoever.

Everybody knew about his current affair, and the prior one, and the one before that, everybody but his wife. Maria didn't really care that he was philandering piece of shit, but the fact that he bent over and spread his cheeks anytime a supervisor from DPD called to complain about their client being mistreated by one of the DVU prosecutors set her off every time. Alan was a lifer at that place, and to leadership, the line prosecutors were expendable. He was never going to go to bat for anyone like Maria. To him, it was more important to appease the judges and DPD supervisors.

A couple of days before, the defendant in one of her cases was released from jail. The court refused to put a no-contact order in place because, in the judge's opinion, the defendant currently lived in another county, did not own a car, and was not likely to encounter the victim. Therefore, the judge opined, a no-contact order was not the least restrictive means for ensuring public safety.

This particular defendant had two convictions in the last three years for violations of domestic violence no-contact orders. He also had two domestic violence assault convictions. He was there that day after being arrested for yet another assault against the same victim. The first two times, the victim had been too scared to assist the prosecution, but on this occasion, she was on board. That fell apart the second the court decided not to issue a no-contact order. The victim knew the defendant would be at her apartment the next day. If she was assisting the prosecutor's office, he would definitely kick the shit out of her. If she refused to assist the prosecutor's office, he might kick the shit out of her.

That's how things work at Seattle Municipal Court. At SMC, judges bow to the defendants and thank them for coming to court. On that day, Judge Derek Johanson delivered his well-worn ridiculous colloquy to the defendant.

"Thank you so much for appearing here in court this morning,

Mr. Lewis. Now, I know how well you were doing after the last time I saw you at your sentencing. You were keeping in contact with your probation officer and had only missed three appointments with her. Now this happens. This is very serious, and I need you to promise that you will stay away from Ms. Thompson. Can you do that? Okay then, I'm going to release you on your promise to appear at your next hearing, and even though I'm not issuing a no-contact order, you might want to stay away from Ms. Thompson, at least until you two can work things out."

This was kangaroo court at its zenith.

Maria sat at counsel table watching the defendant vigorously nod his head, a tiny almost imperceptible grin curling up the corners of his mouth, a perfect example of a microexpression that people are powerless to control. What did his microexpression mean? That was a rhetorical question Maria silently asked herself. She'd been around long enough to know. It meant his victim would have a fat lip an hour after this scumbag was released. Meanwhile, she heard the victim in the gallery behind her sobbing and whimpering "no, no, no" over and over again. His defense attorney, some white Ivy League girl, who'd been in Seattle for about five minutes, went on about how the defendant only had two assault convictions and was trying "really, really hard" to be a good person, but as a person of color, things were extra difficult for him.

The DPD imported these newbie true believers largely from Harvard and Yale. "Who could graduate from an Ivy Leage law school, with hundreds of thousand of dollars in school debt, and then come out to Seattle to slum it at the DPD for $50,000 a year? Rich kids, that's who." The DPD's little army of true believers were the great white hope to all the downtrodden of

Seattle. They came from the cosmopolitan Northeast to the provincial Northwest to spread the good word, just so long as they didn't have to live in Rainier Beach.

"Those fuckers never lived around here either, but they're only too eager to tell everyone who lives in the city how it should run so long as they have a nice little upper-middle-class enclave on the other side of Lake Washington to run to when the sun goes down." As a person of color, Maria was insulted by this dog and pony show these rich little cunts put on in front of the court. Having a privileged white girl sit there with a straight face and tell a white male judge about the adversity faced by people of color was tone-deaf entitlement on a scale few would ever witness, but it was just another day of any week at SMC.

Maria mumbled under her breath, "These uptight white bitches are the most racist people in Seattle."

Maria then addressed the court on the record: "While I'm sure that Yale Law School gave Ms. Spencer over there a great deal of firsthand experience with the sort of adversity that people of color face in the criminal justice system, I should remind the court that the victim in this case is a person of color, as am I. The victim doesn't have any assault convictions, but your whiteness—I mean your honor—and Ms. Karen Snobington Esquire over there are correct. Can we all just give the defendant a big hand for only being convicted of beating the shit out of his girlfriend twice!"

Maria was getting baked in her car before work instead of after, like usual, because she had to attend a meeting to discuss her conduct in court. They couldn't fire her. The city prosecutors had a union and what the law refers to as ownership rights in their public employment. The city continued to inappropriately label the Criminal Division prosecutors as "at will" employees, but in practice, the Civil Division attorneys charged with dealing with the termination of Criminal Division prosecutors knew they were "for cause" employees and proceeded appropriately. The result was an impotent system of progressive discipline.

On the rare occasion that a city department actually did follow through with terminating an employee, the city was always sued by that employee. Shortly thereafter, the Civil Division lawyers in the Employment Unit would roll over at the negotiating table, and the terminated employee would hit soft earth gently after descending on a parachute made of settlement money from the city. At least Seattle was consistent. There were no consequences for defendants and no consequences for city employees. Maria correctly assumed the most entertaining way to coast through a toothless inquiry by two middle-aged white men about her conduct was to do it baked.

Ben knocked on her window. She rolled it down, and a cloud of pot smoke hit him square in the face.

"Did you bring enough for the whole class?" he asked.

Chapter 6

Ben became a middle child around the same time that he became the oldest child. After Mike died, his mother's reaction to her pain was to get pregnant. His parents had met in high school and had stayed together all those years. Ben's mom, Barbara, had gotten pregnant in her senior year of high school. Big Ben and Barbara lived with his parents after high school. Barbara's parents hadn't disowned her or anything, but Big Ben's parents had a finished attic where Big Ben, Barbara, and baby Mike could stay. They stayed long enough for Big Ben to finish his electrician program at Bates Technical College. That was a fancy way of saying vocational or trade school.

Barbara was thirty-nine when she got pregnant with Lisa, Ben's little sister. She wasn't old, but she was pretty old for getting pregnant, especially in the early nineties. Lisa was the baby of a trio of children, the oldest of whom she would never meet. In death, and in her eyes, Mike was the best of big brothers. His story had already been inked. She accepted what was written, and she judged his existence on a rather brief record. Ben, on the other hand, was alive—and fallible.

Ben had been the forgotten child when Mike was alive. Mike took the oxygen out of every room he entered. No one could ever breathe because he had either just impressed you with a talent or skill he possessed or just shocked you with something he'd said or done. In death, Mike loomed large over their home. Ben was now in the middle, smashed between the lionized apple of his parents' eye and their new hope. It seemed unfair to Ben that he was now both the forgotten middle child and the eldest sibling. Eldest sibling came with specific expectations, and by and large, Ben fell short of those expectations.

While he never quite understood, or valued, his role as eldest sibling, he was an excellent forgotten middle child. Does a spare ever really want to be king? Ben never did fill those shoes, and eventually he was permitted to settle into the quiet obscurity he'd always enjoyed within the family unit. It wasn't that his parents neglected him. He knew his parents loved him, that much was clear. After Mike died, Ben mostly operated according to his own agenda. His parents tried to connect with him. They mostly failed, but they tried.

He was lucky because his parents were still married. Most of his friends' parents were divorced. And if they weren't divorced, they couldn't stand each other. Ben's parents were together, and wanted to be together. There wasn't violence, alcoholism, or drug addiction in the home. The family's experience with drug addiction was confined to Mike's crack addiction. If anything was going to drive a wedge between husband and wife, it was the death of a child. Ben's parents didn't split apart. They reinforced each other and propped each other up until they could both stand again.

Ben was effectively trusted to be on his own before Mike died because Mike required so much attention from their parents. Ben was free to be on his own after Mike died because his parents were lost in a fog, and it took some time for them to get their bearings and navigate out of it. Ben remained on his own after Lisa was born because his parents needed to devote their time to a new baby. Ben left the house on his own when he was financially able because he wanted to pursue something other than a blue-collar existence in a gritty little city. Ben was born with the cleverness to manage his own affairs from an early age, and the world obliged him by giving him a largely free hand in crafting his own reality.

He was fourteen, and the area of the backyard that used to be dominated by Ben's fort was now dominated by a four-foot half-pipe. His sophomore effort as a builder was executed with a great deal more precision than the fort. Ben had met this kid Josh earlier that year. They were skating the same spot at the Parkland Transit bus station parking lot. Josh was from Lakewood. Lakewood was effectively an overflow valve for GI housing. It sat right outside Fort Lewis Army Base and McChord Air Force Base. Later, the bases merged and became Joint Base Lewis McChord, but back then it was two separate bases. Every GI who didn't feel like living on base lived in Lakewood, but that wasn't important. Josh's dad had hired someone to build him a half-pipe, and when he was done, he'd given Josh the blueprints he'd drawn up. Josh hung that big piece of drafting paper on his bedroom wall. The first time Ben went to Josh's house, he knew he needed to have that blueprint.

Ben gave Josh twenty bucks for it. After that, he made a list of supplies he needed, went to the hardware store to price it all, and presented the plans and price quote to his dad. Big Ben showed up late from work that Friday evening, his truck loaded down with every item on Ben's price quote list. His dad took him to the garage and showed him where the drill, circular saw, and table saw were. Saturday morning, Ben deconstructed the fort. Sunday morning, Ben started building his ramp. Big Ben came out periodically and assisted on some of the trickier portions. Cutting the transition pieces was especially difficult. Harnessing the metal coping required drilling the steel pipe, and Big Ben mostly took care of that part too. The rest little Ben managed on his own. It was a monument that symbolized his own upward mobility, craftiness, and work ethic.

The first time he dropped in on that half-pipe, he fell flat on his face. For the rest of his life, Ben had the hint of a discolored little scar on his right cheek. The Masonite that covered the half-pipe had left it. It was like the road rash that bikers got when they fell off their motorcycles and the street devoured first their clothing, then their skin. It was a Masonite burn, and he wore it openly with pride. He hadn't been wearing a helmet. He was a street skater, and street skaters wore baseball caps, not helmets. He never started wearing one either. "That ramp had dealt me what I would someday realize was a concussion, but it wasn't my first. Hell, it wasn't my tenth. It certainly wasn't my fuckin' last. I'd been slamming my unprotected head into concrete since that day with Mike at Baker Middle School. By my early twenties, my back was constantly stiff, it hurt to fuckin' stand because my knees were so bad, and I'd had probably a hundred undiagnosed concussions. Honestly, my brain is likely pretty damaged from all the collisions, sort of like a punch-drunk boxer or pro wrestler. It's a wonder I got into any college at all. So what. Suffering ongoing mental issues from undiagnosed head trauma. Whatever. Everybody's carrying around some sort of damage."

Ben knew that people brought their damage to every situation that life presented them. Damage informs future decisions and courses of action. "Nobody can ever be one hundred percent, because to perform at your best means that you've roughed up your body so much that you are likely never better than eighty-five percent, but having the experience that comes from beating yourself to a pulp is what makes you ultimately perform at one hundred and twenty percent. If you're physically a hundred percent, you've never road-tested yourself, so as far as I'm concerned, you're actually sixty percent."

That first ramp concussion rang Ben's bell pretty good. He was dizzy every time he stood up, so he just lay down in the grass. Josh from Lakewood had come out to South Tacoma to give the new ramp a ride. He skated it for about an hour while Ben fell asleep in the grass. After a while, Josh woke Ben up and asked him if he wanted to get high. Ben had taken a couple of puffs off a joint before, but it was shake—just leaves, no buds. Josh held a sticky, smelly little green thing, which had left crystals and orange hairs all over the little dime baggy he pulled it out of. He loaded it into a little steel bowl atop the end of a small steel pipe.

They lay down on the ramp, where no one in the house would see them. After they smoked, they talked and they joked. For a long while they stared at the sky turning orange, then that twilight blue color, and then ultimately that purple that was almost black. Josh grabbed his board and ran off to catch a bus home. Barbara called for Ben to come to dinner sometime later, but he just stayed on the ramp for a while. His mom and dad didn't call for him again. Big Ben told Barbara to let him have fun with his new ramp. Despite the lack of telltale skate noises coming from the ramp, Ben's parents assumed he was out there skating.

Ben looked at his ramp. It was good. It was the product of a defiant and determined personality. Building something required defiance. The temptation to acquiesce, to quit, to beg Big Ben to have somebody more capable come over and build the ramp for him, had dogged him at every turn. He liked Josh, but Ben loathed the idea of having a ramp in his backyard that someone else built.

Skating was great, and building a ramp made him feel good about himself, but the world was composed of much more impressive accomplishments. After he built the ramp, every time he walked to the front of his house, he'd look back and forth. He'd look up and down his little street. Every time he did it, it looked smaller to him. Every time he did it, it felt as if it were closing in on him. When it closed in enough, it would bind him up, tie him down, and ultimately dictate to him the terms of his surrender. It would squash him into that mosaic of pickups and forklifts. It would squash him into that city of socially undervalued vocational trade skills. It would squash him into that honest but limited view of the world.

He started wondering if he'd been hoodwinked. Ben never tried at school. He could be lazy when it suited his purposes, even more so when it would irritate someone. He'd thought that fucking around at school was defiance. Right then he became convinced that he'd been duped. School wasn't there for people like him to succeed. It was the appearance of social mobility, but there was no incentive for schools to produce upwardly mobile people in percentages greater than society's need for them. Society needed only a small percentage of people to be educated and capable. In fact, society needed most people to stay ignorant and lazy. His middle school needed him to stay right where society had placed him. His middle school needed to produce academic failures in much greater numbers than they did academic successes.

By fucking around in school, he was doing exactly what he was designed to do, which was to stay put. To leave the socioeconomic strata he'd been born into was society's nightmare. To succeed in spite of overwhelming opposition was true defiance. That Monday, Ben did something that he'd never done before. He went to school and turned in a homework assignment on time.

Chapter 7

Erin O'Connell worked for the DPD. More specifically, she worked for The Defender Association, a particularly zealous division of public defenders within the DPD. If you said TDA, everyone around there knew what you meant. Burning down every prosecutor's office in the county, along with the prosecutors inside, appeared to be TDA's sole purpose for existing. They were good at it, too, certainly the tip of the spear, or the green berets of the DPD. From Ben's perspective, they used their clients as battering rams and cannon fodder on the front lines of ideological legal campaigns designed to dismantle the system, brick by brick if necessary. But Ben was a prosecutor, so it's possible that his impression may have been a little less than objective.

Prior to working at TDA, Erin actually admired, even venerated, TDA and the DPD more generally for their steadfast determination to get justice for the most disadvantaged people in our society. After three years at TDA, she was a war-weary soldier who was just trying to keep her compass pointed to true north. Day after day she put on her armor, picked up her sword, and set out to slay the dragon. She was a good soldier too. If the DPD said to go take a hill, she took that hill, but she wasn't a true believer. A good soldier, yes, but in like-minded company, during interludes of momentary candor, she voiced her concerns.

DPD soldiers didn't typically spend three years in the misdemeanor trenches. By the time they had a year, they would promote out of municipal court. They would go to superior court, still rank and file but in charge of defending felony cases instead of the petty misdemeanors in muni court. Sometimes they'd become supervisors in muni court. More often than not, they'd end up as casualties, departing the battlefield altogether.

Erin was an aberration and, in all honesty, a thorn in the side of her division. That first year, all the newbie DPD attorneys were born into the practice as Kool-Aid drinkers. The DPD preferred to get fresh law school grads. They combed Ivy League job fairs looking for the perfect marks. Their meat was rich kids carrying around three tons of white guilt, charged up by the idea of bringing a superior brand of justice to the far-flung reaches of provincial nowhere cities such as Seattle. To that tune, they enlisted. Like the missionaries of old, they marched into the savage terrain of places like the Pacific Northwest to civilize the land with New England aristocratic values. They marched with a criminal code book in one hand, the new word of God—not a bible, just the new white law.

Like a new-model Christian soldier, Erin marched right out of Harvard Law and into the fray. She was a good Protestant girl from New England, so of course she marched. She was a WASP of the first order. Her parents were old money, New England proper, Dover. Of course she marched out of Harvard Law and not, say, BU Law. BU is where all the blue-collar lawyers went. They were the poor Catholics from Southie who crawled out of the grime and shit of the gutter to gain an inkling of respectability by becoming prosecutors in the Suffolk County

District Attorney's Office. Erin rightly figured that nobody from BU Law ever left Boston. Most of them probably never even found work as lawyers at all. Certainly, nobody from Seattle was at their law school's job fairs trying to recruit them to their righteous cause.

Because of her pedigree, Erin never had a meaningful choice about where she would go to college. There was an expectation that it was going to be Harvard or Yale. The binary choice presented to her was about as interesting as the choice between Coke and Pepsi. Given the opportunity, she would have gone to the University of California at Berkeley. She could have gotten in, but it wasn't an option for her. In her family, going to a hippie school on the West Coast was strictly forbidden. That was especially true when talking about a state school. The only West Coast option in her family was Stanford, and Stanford would only have been an option for her if she were mentally slow.

Her parents spent thousands on SAT prep courses for her. They also hired a lawyer to harass the illustrious Groton School into changing three of Erin's B grades to A grades, so as not to besmirch her Harvard and Yale applications. Being captain of Groton's tennis team and volunteering at the local food bank rounded out her applications. Putting together those applications was just an assembly-line operation in her community. Everybody knew what needed to be there. Smarts, sports, and service—it was the holy trinity of Ivy League applications.

Since she planned to go to law school, she chose the easiest college major she could find: communications. The plan was to get the highest GPA possible, and that was most readily accomplished by taking the easiest classes offered. Surprisingly, getting great grades at an Ivy League school was not hard. Maybe they figured if you could pay the tuition, you were entitled to the grade. Much the same way, in times gone by, men assumed if they bought a woman dinner and took her to a movie, they'd essentially purchased use of the woman's body at the end of the evening.

Maybe these schools just didn't want to admit that their handpicked crops of spoiled silver-spoon whiners were largely nothing more than kids of average intellect with superior funding. "For Christ's sake, George W. Bush when to Yale. After that, he went to Harvard Business School when he couldn't get into a state law school. How hard can those curriculums be if a bonehead like W graduated from them?"

It wasn't even their fault, but most of them were truly nothing more than toy robots. Their parents would wind them up and point them toward their goals. Parents who didn't even bother to take a primary role in raising their children in the first place became very active when the discussion turned toward reaffirming their own narcissism by wedging their offspring into Ivy League schools. Erin was certainly used to the shuffle. Her prep school's tuition was more than the tuition at most private colleges. She lived in a dormitory all week long, and went home to Dover on the weekends and holidays. She didn't have to work hard to get good grades in high school, and her dad's lawyer fixed the ones she couldn't achieve herself. In similar fashion, Erin cruised through Yale's undergraduate curriculum as well.

After college, she took a whole year off just to study for the LSAT. Getting into Harvard or Yale required, in addition to an impeccable undergrad GPA, an LSAT score of at least 175 out of a possible 180. Her internship at the New Haven Legal

Assistance Association and being on Yale's women's tennis team, coupled with her 177 LSAT score and 3.94 GPA, pretty well assured her acceptance to Harvard or Yale Law.

Harvard Law turned out to be just another link on the long chain of formality heavy but substance devoid activities. There was much to hear but little to learn. Erin's grades remained very good, though not 3.94 GPA good. By the end of her first semester, she realized that there was no school to get into after law school. She didn't have to engage in any extracurricular activities because there were no more school applications to be filled out. Even if she graduated dead last in her class, her future was assured. There would be a bar exam to pass, but the reality of the situation was that she would be a Harvard Law School graduate, and as such, there was nobody left to impress.

Jumping through the hoops set out by her family hadn't really bothered her. She was a good show pony, and she could perform ad nauseam. It bothered her that, at the end of it, she had done little more than attain the bare minimum expected by her family. Going to Harvard Law School, graduating near the top of her class, these things didn't set her apart. They only ensured her continued trajectory toward the upper class, the crown made from Ben Franklins, the only royalty the United States permitted: the Moneyarchy.

As soon as she realized there was nothing she could ever do to impress anyone in her orbit, she decided to take a summer internship with the DPD in Seattle. It wasn't California, but she had figured that a summer on the West Coast would be a welcome change of pace from buttoned-down and tied-up New England. "I used to think she meant 'tied up' like they were stitched into their lifestyle by money and class, but then she told me she always said 'buttoned-down and tied-up' because

New England was full of closet BDSM freaks. I guess if you're that stifled in your normal life, the freaky shit's got to come out somewhere, and apparently that's it. Erin told me about all the sex-dungeon gear she'd found in her parents' private room, weird shit too: leather underwear, whips, ball gags, you know, normal uptight New Englander stuff."

After that first summer in Seattle, Erin came back after her 2L year, and accepted a job offer after graduation, pending passage of the Washington State bar exam, of course. Unlike every other standardized test she'd taken before, she wasn't shooting for the top 5 percent of scores. It was the first time in her life that the score really didn't matter as long as she passed. Nobody ever asked you what you scored on your bar exam. She took a bar prep course early that summer and passed the exam with ease.

Erin slayed many a dragon that first year at the DPD. By the end of it, she began to realize that many of her baby lawyer colleagues had disappeared from the DPD altogether. People with similar blue-chip pedigrees had abandoned the law as a profession after a brutal year at the DPD. New ones showed up by the dozens as soon as summer bar scores were posted. This ritual first-year massacre was not something widely talked about at the DPD, certainly not by the supervisors.

For the first time since being at the DPD, there was a chink in Erin's armor as she observed the smiling mask worn by her DPD minder, Tim Hathaway, absorb its first crack when she questioned him about this exodus. When Erin began voicing concerns about client outcomes versus superfluous litigation designed to thwart the courts and prosecutors' offices and change the political landscape through appellate litigation, the second crack in Tim's mask appeared. Water seeped in, and those cracks swelled over the ensuing two years to the point where Erin could see a much more sinister smile on the face of her mask-laden minder.

From that point on, she was a liability to her division and to the DPD as a whole. She took her orders and she executed them, but she was a dissident. She did the bare minimum of the political agenda pushing required by the DPD, and focused extra hours above and beyond what was required on client outcomes.

More importantly, she stopped viewing her clients as angels with dirty faces and started seeing them as they were. Sometimes they were people suffering from a mental health or substance use issue and committing petty crimes as a result of that affliction. Sometimes they were dumb, barely adult teenagers making bad decisions. Sometimes they were hardened criminals committing petty crimes as a matter of course, just an ongoing consequence of their being alive. Taking off the rose-colored glasses made her a much more effective public defender. She began seeking the appropriate resolution to her clients' criminal matters instead of fighting with the prosecutors and courts simply for the purpose of fighting.

She was a better lawyer, that much was indisputable. Her clients' outcomes were better and more appropriate in light of their circumstances. But as a dissident, she was a grotesque perversion and thus wished into the cornfield.

Chapter 8

On the other side of the bog, a young Benjamin Sullivan stared blankly at a blackboard with a string of numbers, letters, and symbols on it. It was an AP Calculus class at Mount Tahoma High School in South Tacoma. While he was staring at the blackboard, he decided to start calling the neighborhood Southie Tacoma. People from around there called it South T, but Ben thought his play on Southie in Boston was clever. He decided he would try to get it circulating through his group of friends. Hopefully, it would spread from there. The city as a whole was already pretty well supplied with good nicknames. There was T-Town and, of course, Tacomatose, aka the greatest nickname for a city ever. It had a slogan now, too: "Tacoma 185,000 Alcoholics Can't Be Wrong." That one had shown up on a T-shirt recently, and Ben kept meaning to get one but never did.

Right then, Ben's teacher called on him to provide an answer to the equation on the board. Ben was in the AP Calculus class because he had been planning on going into a math-based discipline in college. He was good at fixing things—cars, appliances, anything mechanical. He didn't want to be a mechanic, though. He thought he might become an engineer. He understood algebra. He was even good at it. Geometry was practical, almost as practical as basic arithmetic. Normal people could use geometry to solve all sorts of everyday problems. Trigonometry was a little more esoteric, but he still got a B in it. He could see its usefulness for what he was interested in, even if it had a very diminished level of usefulness for most normal people.

It was day three of AP Calculus, and Ben had an epiphany in two parts when his teacher called on him that day. First, calculus was a necessary skill for any engineer to master. Second, Ben would never master it. "Basically, I just said I didn't feel well. My teacher moved on to some other poor student, this girl who looked as confused as I was. Too bad for her."

Getting into an engineering program at the University of Washington would be impossible without stellar grades in advanced math courses. "Trig was hard, but I gutted out a B. I would have passed AP calc, but I probably would have gotten a C, which would have put an end to my aspirations of going into a math-based discipline. Even if I had managed to get into an engineering program at some other university, with a C in AP calc, the college-level courses in any engineering program anywhere would have ground me out of college altogether. That, or I would have ended up with a bachelor's in something useless like communications."

A tall, goofy-looking motherfucker with a cartoonishly huge revolver once said, "A man's got to know his limitations." "That goofy-looking motherfucker was right about that. He was wrong about what revolver to carry—a .44 mag, seriously? A .357 mag has all the stopping power anyone could ever need, plus you can actually hit what you're aiming at. A .44 mag kicks like a fuckin' mule. You're lucky if you can hit the side of a moving van. No wonder he had to use all six shots in *Dirty Harry*. Whatever. Keep dreamin', Clint!"

It was the last semester of Ben's senior year, and he was within the drop window. Even with all the math classes, he'd managed to keep his GPA in the 3.8 neighborhood, and since he was dropping out of AP Calculus, he decided to take a class he genuinely wouldn't have to work hard at. In the school office, he looked at the list of classes that hadn't filled up. There were still two open spots in the drama class, so he signed up. Little did he know how useful the skills taught in that class would ultimately be to him in his adult profession.

Before that day, Ben had a clear direction. There had been a pinprick of light coming at him through the construction paper of life. All that had been required of him at any given moment was to continue to move toward that little point of light in whatever fashion he was able. Going to college was still the plan, and going to the University of Washington was his highest aspiration.

Applying anywhere else didn't even occur to Ben. Small-town thinking and a townie-centric mindset prevented Ben from thinking outside the part of the I-5 corridor that encapsulated Olympia to the south, Tacoma in the center, and Seattle to the north. And in that little snow globe of existence, one university sat high above the rest, U-dub. Ben's provincialism moved backward and forward through time, so much so that to say that he was born, lived, and would die within view of the Puget Sound would be more or less accurate.

When he did arrive at U-dub the following fall, he was amazed to discover that many of his fellow students were not just from all around the country but from all around the world. Similarly, the fact that many of his professors went to

Ivy League schools back east also came as a surprise. Up until that point, he had just assumed that the professors had gone to U-dub themselves.

Before that first day of class, he'd thought only presidents and Supreme Court justices went to Harvard or Yale. To him, they weren't even colleges, they were hidden realms. They were places that people talked about but nobody ever actually saw, much less attend. His family wasn't exactly the traveling to the east coast type. Even if they had gone to Boston or New Haven, they wouldn't have been meandering around an Ivy League university's campus. Either way, they hadn't, and he didn't. Later, as an adult, when he went to New York City and Boston for the first time, he saw not only that these fantastical places were indeed real but that they had entire systems of medieval serfs servicing them.

Harvard and MIT might have their share of geniuses, but as far as Ben could tell, Boston was full of dum-dums. New Haven wasn't even a city so much as an overworked teat that Yale sucked dry with insistent regularity. "Walking around those campuses took all the magic outta those places for me. Before I visited, they were these mythical institutions, pumping out the next generation of America's elite. They certainly pump out the next generation of America's elite, but not the way that you think. They're grooming facilities for persons born into a certain caste. The king doesn't dress himself. The king has never dressed himself. The king cannot dress himself."

Other than lording over their army of undereducated blue-collar white kids at the cafeteria, berating the Puerto Rican women who clean their dorms, or screaming at the Black gardener while they're canoodling on the quad, Ben wasn't sure what exactly students at these places did. At U-dub, students worked part-time jobs in the evenings and studied on the weekends. So far as Ben could tell, Ivy League students went to one of the campus bars in the evenings and to the ski lodge on the weekends. As ever, bourgeois ease and comfort exist because of working-class sweat. "Say what you will, but Ivy League life certainly prepares one for a life as the master of a South Carolina plantation in the eighteenth century. Now bow to the people whose lives your labor makes possible."

Ben didn't know all that yet. He hadn't realized that he was at the beginning of a cycle, a cycle that his counterparts at the DPD were at the end of. Those Ivy Leaguers at the DPD had risen to the pinnacle of their ability. They had achieved all that the descendants of descendants of descendants of someone with a creative spark could accomplish. For them, at some point a hard-working ancestor had toiled to put a child through college. That child did, or created something that no one had before. That child's children reaped the benefits of that novel idea. Those people's children were so far removed from that original spark of genius but so bathed in its wealth that they lost the ability to think interesting thoughts and instead focused their attention on class and status. Those people's children became so decadent that they believed in their own superiority, despite their being quite average in most respects. Those people's children, or the ones who come after them, will be so far removed from the original wealth and privilege of their bloodline that they will multiply and disperse, live and learn more modestly. Their lives will become average, and their children will live average lives. Some will even become working-class, and undereducated. Then the machine will be ready for another spark from someone unique, appearing in the hoi polloi of society.

The natural rise and fall of all things, the recycling of human experience, when put into perspective, turns the elite into an average commodity and turns Ben into a unique and scarce resource. Big Ben had pushed the door open for him, and a unique quirk of the mind coupled with a Rainier tall boy worth of tenacity and courage propelled Ben out of his class. He achieved that most illusive of illusive things in American society: social mobility. Banging around somewhere in his head, unbeknownst to him, was an idea no one had ever had, or an adaptation on life that would eventually change the trajectory of his own bloodline. Someday he would have spoiled-rotten mush-brained great-grandchildren that he couldn't stand, and those great-grandchildren most certainly would go to Harvard or Yale—or both if they were as dumb as George W. Bush.

But he didn't know all that yet.

Chapter 9

For Ben, it was the night of his high school graduation. He was invited to a couple of after-graduation parties. He was well-liked at Mount Tahoma High School. The popular kids—jocks, cheerleaders, and the like—all welcomed him. They were popular at a public high school in a beat-up little city. Tonight was their swan song. Tomorrow they'd be nobody. They were actually nobody all along, but high school had cloaked that fact from them. Ben didn't like them, not a one. He didn't hate them either. They were just who they were, and Ben wasn't whatever that was, even if they wanted him to be. He knew the star wrestler, Matt, would go to some vocational school, marry a girl from Tacoma, and have some kids. Matt was Ben's dad, just thirty years later.

After the graduation ceremony, Big Ben, Barbara, Ben, and Ben's little Lisa had dinner at Johnny's Dock. Johnny's is what passed for a nice restaurant in Tacoma. The parties weren't getting started until eight or nine, and he had plenty of time to get to some or even all of them. He didn't. He blew off those graduation parties. Since graduation day was the last time he'd purposely see anyone he went to high school with, he didn't see the point of drawing it out by going to any of their parties.

Graduation family dinner was just like any other fancy family dinner. It was more for Ben's parents than for him. They deserved a nice meal. They'd gotten a kid over the first major hurdle of life. After dinner, Big Ben gave Ben the keys to a beautifully restored 1965 Plymouth Barracuda. It was midnight blue, had Crager five-spoke chrome rims, and that fastback wraparound rear window. Big Ben had been restoring it in his buddy's garage for months. He'd been working on it most evenings and every weekend.

Big Ben had met them at Johnny's, and he'd driven the Barracuda. Barbara and Lisa were already in the Camry when Big Ben leaned into the driver's-side window of the Barracuda, where Ben was running his hand over the freshly Armor All'd dashboard.

"U-dub is in Seattle, kid. Now, if you wind up moving to the dorms up there, you got a way to get back down here to visit us. And trust me when I tell you that you will visit us."

Big Ben motioned like he was breaking something over his knee and pointed at Ben while he spoke.

"Don't get fucked up and drive tonight either, kid. That fuckin' car took months to restore. If you're going to get drunk and smash somethin' up, take that shit box over there your mom calls a car."

"Thanks, pap. I'll behave."

"I love you, kid."

"I know. I'm gonna take off."

Ben had never driven anything but his mom's Camry, his dad's truck, and the driver's ed car. The Barracuda was a stick. His dad's truck was a stick, so he knew how to drive it, but it wasn't second nature yet. He pushed the clutch in. Johnny's parking lot was relatively empty, and the asphalt was wet, so he floored the gas pedal and popped his foot off the clutch. The rear tires spun so hard that the car lost traction and started to skid. He let off the accelerator a little and steered out of the inevitable donut. From that moment on, he pretty well had the hang of the stick.

On his way out of the parking lot, Ben glanced over and saw Big Ben standing next to Barbara's Camry with his arms folded, watching Ben, shaking his head. Ben leaned on the horn as a final adios to his family.

The first place Ben went was the Lucky 7 on Ninth and MLK. It wasn't the best spot to stop. It was right where Mike had been shot. In all honesty, even six years later, it was still mostly an open-air crack market. But they sold beer to teenagers, so it was a necessary first stop. He grabbed a six-pack of Rainier tall boys. He was heading over to Josh's to pick him up and go to a show. Ben wasn't interested in getting wasted. He just wanted to drink a few beers so he could have a buzz at the show. Plus, he knew Josh would have weed. He figured Josh would drink a couple of the Rainiers. That would keep Ben from getting too drunk. The weed would wear off long before he had to drive home, all nice and safe, just like Big Ben said.

The Paradox was in this old single-story building on Puyallup Avenue. Ben wasn't sure what it used to be, but it was so beat down, old, and nasty, he knew it had been something else at some point. Six months earlier, it had been no place, boarded up for who knows how long. All punk venues opened up in some dilapidated purposeless shack. That place fit the bill exactly.

It sat in the shade of the Tacoma Dome, straddled between the dome and the downtown side of Commencement Bay. Ben wasn't sure, but his best guess was that the Paradox building used to be a fish-processing plant or some sort of minimal consumer goods distribution center. Most of the buildings down there had, at some point, been a cog in the Port of Tacoma's massive system of logistics. The port was outsized to say the least. It was one of the defining characteristics of Tacoma, that and all the GIs. Despite being a quarter of Seattle's size, Tacoma's port was nearly as large as the massive Port of Seattle. Sixty years ago, trucks would have brought goods to a building like this one, where they'd be unloaded manually by longshoremen. There they'd sit until another truck came along and picked up this or that to go cross-country to its final destination. There were now much larger distribution centers outside of town and much larger trucks, and, because of automation, a much smaller army of longshoremen. When you added the logging industry into the other distribution chain job losses, it was easy to see how western Washington had become a sort of ground zero for blue-collar plight and socioeconomic depression.

A few of years before that, the Warped Tour had been up at the Tacoma Dome parking lot. Josh and Ben had been skating downtown. They had been kids, really kids, teenagers not even old enough to drive. They barely had money for the bus to get downtown, much less go to the show. Sometimes they'd just skate to downtown, since half of the ride was downhill. Since half the return trip was up the same hill, they always kept bus money for the ride home.

That bus money was all they had on them as they sat outside the Texaco on Pacific Avenue down the road from the dome. This girl with Manic Panic fire-engine red hair was walking toward the gas station parking lot. She was being followed by this jock in a Camaro. He was lobbing lewd comments at her, and it wasn't clear if he wanted to fuck her or kill her. Either way, Ben had picked up a rock and thrown it right at the

Camaro's windshield. It had spider-webbed it beautifully upon impact.

That Brian Bosworth–looking jock had slammed the Camaro into park and gotten out. Josh and Ben started toward the Camaro with their boards raised into bludgeoning position. All skaters know that a skateboard is not just your recreation and mode of transportation but also a deadly weapon. Faced with two feral teenagers and a now emboldened and angry young woman, Camaro man retreated. That young woman was in a band—no one Ben or Josh had ever heard of, but it was on the Warped Tour lineup—and as a thank-you, she gave Josh and Ben free passes.

Ben pulled up to the curb at D Street about a block away from the Paradox. He heard the front passenger-side rim scrape the curb, and he was relieved. Anytime he got something new, he could never relax until it got its first scar. The need to keep possessions pristine was a curse, one that Ben suffered from. That first scratch on a new skateboard deck hurt him emotionally, but it also started a process of acceptance that always resulted in the ability to use the possession in the manner in which it was intended. A board was meant to be ridden. Scratching it on a curb was kind of the point. A car was meant to be driven. Scraping the rims on a curb was inevitable. All was as it was meant to be. Ben exhaled.

High school graduation was a transition time for lots of people. At his school, most of those people were having a last hurrah at some after-graduation party. Josh lived in Lakewood, so they didn't go to the same school. Josh had graduated that day too. Neither of them was missing anyone or anything from high school that night, and nobody from high school was likely missing them.

They drank a few Rainiers and smoked a few bowls before heading into the show. They sat in the Barracuda so long they missed most of the opening bands. "No harm done. No loss there. Most of those openers were kids our age in bands that could barely play, but we made it in for the Psychedelic Razors." They played about ten songs in like eleven minutes. Then they just walked off the stage. Everyone in the crowd was silent. Nobody had seen anything like it before. This wall of noise just came at you and entertained your ears by violently smashing into your eardrums repeatedly. Then it was gone, just like the band, gone. "Well, not really gone; they had bolted to the door at the side of the stage and were loading their gear. They were clearly in a hurry to get the fuck out of there. They didn't even bring any merchandise to sell."

Outside, Ben could see the singer under the streetlight by their van. There wasn't much light in the Paradox. During their set, he could tell that the singer was a girl, but that was about it. Under the streetlight, he could properly see this little female powder keg who had exploded her voice all over a crowd of Tacoma punks.

She was a little Latina girl, maybe twenty-one. Her eyes were blackened all around with makeup that extended to fading vertical points continuing north and south of her eyes. She had on tight black jeans that were peg-stitched up to the knees, a denim vest with crusty punk band patches all over it, and loosely dreaded shoulder-length black hair.

"I knew they had a seven-inch because I saw it at Mother Records, but I didn't get it because I didn't know if they were any good. I figured if I liked them, I'd get it at the show, but they didn't bring any fuckin' records to sell, or anything else like T-shirts either. I asked the singer girl if they had any of the seven-inches."

She just pulled out this little journal and tore a corner off one of the pages. She wrote down a phone number and a name, "Maria." She capitalized the *A* and drew a circle around it so that it looked like an anarchy symbol. "It was a weird number, though, a 509 area code. I didn't know where 509 was. I thought maybe it was Portland or Idaho, eastern Washington maybe? I was pretty sure they were a Seattle band, so I figured she must have written down an old number, or wrote it down wrong, or maybe she was just giving me a bogus number? Whatever, I don't know. I found that slip of paper with her number on it crammed into one of my record sleeves years later. And it wasn't even in a Psychedelic Razors record—it was some other band's record sleeve. And I never got a copy of that one seven-inch of theirs either."

The little powder keg singer looked at Ben and said, "We ran out of seven-inches. We're printing more. Call me in a few days, and I'll tell you when we're going to have more."

After that, she and the rest of the band jumped into their van so quick it was like they'd been practicing getting away from a bank heist. Then she was gone.

Chapter 10

Maria wasn't from Seattle. To be honest, she didn't know where she was from. One upon a time, her parents were farmworkers. Her father, Juan, was a migrant farmworker. He typically left Washington by the end of August and was back by June. Her father and her mother, Luisa, were married, always had been. Maria had a sister and a brother. Three was the right number of children for a family like theirs, plenty of hands to pitch in and work but not so many that it was a burden to feed them. Plus, there was enough of them to keep one another company.

Maria and her siblings were citizens, as was Luisa. Juan was not a citizen, and due to several illegal entries into the United States, he never would be. In fact, he was permanently barred from citizenship, permanent residence status, or even going on vacation in the states. In the Yakima Valley, if you stayed for the summer, nobody—not the cops, not INS—ever bothered you. You were an integral part of the agricultural economy, which was the lifeblood of eastern Washington. However, if you were illegal and showed up before things started to bloom or stayed until the leaves on the trees started to turn brown, you were in for trouble. Everybody in town knew who was legal and who was illegal, who stayed all year round and who arrived with the sun.

Luisa had been born in the Yakima Valley, born on a kitchen table in the house in which she would eventually raise her own family, if one was to believe the family stories. Her father had been a migrant farmworker, ranch hand, mechanic, jack-of-all-trades. Her mother was a citizen, born to migrant farmworkers. Luisa's parents had come to the Yakima Valley in the fifties for work. Much like Maria's father, Luisa's father spent most of the year traveling for work—and to stay one step ahead of the authorities. In the winter, he'd lay low in Juarez, his city of origin. After their third year in the Yakima Valley, two pivotal things happened to Luisa's parents. First, they secured a bank loan to purchase the house where Maria and her siblings would be raised. Second, Luisa was born.

The house was sacred, as it was social proof—a calling card denoting permanence and belonging. Of course, it had to be purchased in Maria's grandmother's name, as her grandfather was illegal. The simple ranch house had a little farm-style fence that was good for nothing more than marking the property line. It was practically new when Maria's grandparents bought it, not so much by the time Maria and her siblings were growing up in it.

When he was away, her grandfather sent letters and money home at least once a month, every month he was away—until he didn't. This wasn't just a story she'd been told; the letters were in a cabinet in the living room. When Maria was little, she used to look at the postmarked stamps and wonder what her grandfather was doing in Caprock, New Mexico, in November 1957 or in Elgin, Arizona, in February 1961. The letters were sweet. Her grandfather always closed with "Love to you and little Luisa."

Those letters also revealed something important about her grandfather. He would routinely write about what a comfort it was to him that he never had to wonder where his family was and always knew where home was, even if he couldn't be there most of the time. It seemed clear to Maria that her grandfather, from afar, took almost as much pride in having a permanent address in the United States, as he did from having the house itself. While the letters themselves were written with a very relaxed hand, their home address on the envelope was written very clearly, very purposefully, never sloppy. Having that home for his family was of paramount importance to him, even though he could never step foot in it without being effectively outside the law. His greatest comfort was having a nap on his favorite chair, surrounded by his wife and daughter, in a home he could never legally inhabit.

One month, no letter arrived. The last letter in the cabinet is postmarked November 1965. There was no December 1965 letter, and there were no letters from 1966 at all—or any year after that. If her grandfather's pattern over the previous years had held true, he would have been in Juarez in December 1965. Maria's grandmother had sent letters to the couple of addresses she had for her grandfather's family in Juarez, but there was no response. Of course, receiving a response would have been miraculous, as in a city like Juarez, there was little chance that any of her grandfather's family had the same address as they'd had years before.

One way or the other, at least for them, her grandfather's story ended right there. If it had been someone else, any other man, Maria would have figured he'd met another woman, started a new life. That didn't square with the man she'd come to know from his letters. That home, his wife, their daughter, had been a light at the end of a monthslong tunnel that he traveled every year just to get back to them for a few months. During the growing season in Yakima, he worked a minimum of twelve hours most days, but delighted in the couple of hours he was able to spend with them before showering and collapsing into an exhausted sleep coma.

After he was gone, Maria's grandmother worked more and kept up the house payments. When school let out in June, little Luisa picked fruits and vegetables at this farm or that, in order to augment the small amount of income in the house. When Luisa was a teenager, she met Juan. He was in his mid-twenties but had already been permanently barred from reentry into the United States, meaning that he lived much like Maria's grandfather.

Maria was born in 1978, and her siblings arrived in rapid succession after that. When Maria was eleven, her grandmother had a heart attack. She didn't go to the hospital right away because she didn't have any medical insurance and was worried about bringing a financial burden on the family. Apparently, the heart attack was fairly mild, and her grandmother sincerely believed it was just some bug or indigestion. Two days later, an ambulance picked up Maria's grandmother after it was clear she was very ill. She expired on the way to the hospital. She had recently made the final payment on the house, and the deed had come in the mail a few months after that. Maria's grandmother lived a total of eleven months in a house that she, not the bank, owned.

So, to the best of Maria's thinking, she was from Yakima. Her grandmother, grandfather, mother, and father had each surmounted mountain-sized obstacles to ensure that she and her siblings could be from Yakima, in the United States, so that's where she was from.

Being a natural-born US citizen and the descendant of migrant illegals came with certain expectations. Maria had never picked a fruit or vegetable in her life. When Maria was growing up, Luisa was a grocery checker at the Safeway near their house, a union job. Juan sent money home when he was out of town and brought home his paycheck when he was in Yakima. By that time, Juan was a carpenter and handyman. The little ranch house was paid for, and each of the kids had their own room. So little Maria studied. She couldn't be idle, not even if she wanted to be; it wasn't in her genes. Her parents and grandparents had kicked the door open for her, and now she had to walk through it.

After high school, her first stop was Gonzaga University, a few hours east down I-90. College was an esoteric concept to her parents, but without ever stepping foot on a university campus, Juan and Luisa knew they wanted their children to go. To them, it was like the yellow-brick road—and Gonzaga University was the Jesuit Catholic city on a hill. It appeared to be the path to the promised land, even if they lacked a clear picture of what the promised land actually was. But it wasn't for them to find out; it was for them to be the bricks in the wall that supported the next highest brick, and Maria's grandparents had been the bricks supporting Luisa, and so on and so forth. The fact that Maria was studying at a Jesuit Catholic university fulfilled for Juan and Luisa all the aspirations they'd had for themselves as parents.

But what does a little Latina girl from farm country do after college? Her parents and younger siblings, one of which was a sophomore at WSU by that point, thought that a bachelor's degree in English was the only credential necessary to get a six-figure job in the city. That's what Maria thought on her first day of college too. It didn't take long to figure out that all her professors had PhDs, and that everybody with money had a professional degree. Lawyers, architects, doctors, these were the high earners.

College had effectively given her the necessary credentials to get an entry-level job in some anonymous office tower in Seattle. That prestigious honor was augmented by her ability to afford a one-bedroom apartment in a low-rise turn-of-the-century brick apartment building on Capitol Hill called the Gayle.

The move to Seattle was hard. Seattle was actually closer to Yakima than Spokane was, but for some reason Gonzaga didn't seem like it was far away from home. Spokane had a similar feel to Yakima, despite the fact that it was much larger. Spokane was by far the largest city she'd ever lived in up to that point. Before Seattle, she'd only ever lived in two places: Yakima and Spokane.

Seattle may have been closer, but it was on the other side of a mountain range that sprawled upward so high that sometimes when you were near it, you'd have to look straight up to even see where the sky began. The geographic hurdle was still somehow lower than the cultural one. She wasn't conservative politically. She was the singer in a hardcore band, for Christ's sake, but somehow railing against all the Republicans in Yakima and Spokane seemed more comfortable than dealing with the counterculture weirdos in Seattle. She should have fit right in, but she was a small-town punk girl, and everyone she met in Seattle seemed as though they'd grown up there.

The guitarist from her band went to Seattle as well. The bass player and drummer stayed in Spokane and started another forgettable band. Once they were settled, she and Adam—the Psychedelic Razor's guitar player—began their search for a new bass player and drummer. In Seattle in the year 2000, finding a punk-rock drummer couldn't have been easier. They put a handwritten notice on the corkboard at the Vivace café on Broadway. By the next day, they had three would-be drummers. They didn't choose the most talented one, because he was pretty arrogant. They didn't choose the worst guy, either, because he was objectively terrible. Maria was convinced that he had borrowed some drums and, never having played them before, taught himself "Tequila" an hour before the audition. And he couldn't even play *that* properly. For Maria and Adam, at least for the time being, the middle guy would do. A decent bass player was a little harder to locate, but by the end of the week, the Psychedelic Razors were up and running.

For a couple of years, that life suited her. As far as her parents and sibling were concerned, she was a rock star. In reality, she had to beg club owners to let the band play, and she made so little money that all she could afford was a latte at Vivace for breakfast and two cheeseburgers and fries at Dick's for dinner. She always skipped lunch, but somehow she was still broke most of the time.

Over the next few years, the Psychedelic Razors petered out. In the late nineties, the Murder City Devils changed the punk landscape in Seattle, effectively remaking the city's music scene in their own image. Their evolution away from sixty-second songs to something a little more blues and rock and roll severely dampened the aspirations of bands that still prayed at the altar of holy hardcore. The Razors cut a few more seven-inch records, on a few forgettable small record labels. In 2001, the year before they called it quits, they self-released a discography on CD and did a two-month US tour. Maria returned to Seattle with eighty-two dollars—her part of the "profit" from the tour. She'd taken a leave of absence from work, but upon her return, it became quite clear that they didn't require, or desire, her return.

Her life as a musician was beyond over, and she mourned her lost stardom. Not that singers from hardcore bands craved fame, but any notoriety and recognition would now forever elude her. She was late on rent because of the tour. Now that she'd finally settled into the city, she was terrified that her life as a Seattleite was close to being over. She had fucking hated her job, so while she had no idea how she was going to make a living, she cheered the demise of her life as a downtown cubicle drone.

On that Monday, she picked up her tiny and insignificant possessions from her cubicle, as well as her last paycheck. She used the overwhelming majority of her check to get current on her rent. On Tuesday, she walked to the Kinkos on Roy Street and made several copies of a flyer seeking a roommate. She walked to the Vivace and tacked up one of the flyers on the corkboard. When she went up to the counter to order her latte, she spied something new: a sign that read "Help Wanted."

Chapter 11

It was the year 2000, and at some point in recent years, people coming of age around the beginning of the millennium began being referred to as millennials, or Gen Y. Ben was born in 1981, so as best as he could figure, he was Gen X. But being born at the end of 1981, he had much more in common with older millennials then he did with Gen Xers born in the sixties. Was he the last Gen Xer born, or was he the first millennial ever? Was he welcome in either tribe, or rejected by both? Forever in-between here and there was Ben's lot in life.

The acute aloofness that the world had exhibited toward him was all the more obvious that first quarter at U-dub. U-dub filled a particular niche in American culture. It was effectively an Ivy League university, professionally camouflaged as a public university. It wasn't just that it had a great medical school and a first-class university hospital, or even that it had multiple Nobel laureates on the faculty. It wasn't that it had amazing architecture and stellar science programs. It wasn't that it had a great law school. It wasn't the huge endowment or the active and noteworthy alumni. It wasn't the enormous, well-manicured campus grounds, or the corporately sponsored state-of-the-art facilities all over that well-manicured campus.

It wasn't the ridiculously well-funded football program and its fourteen Rose Bowl appearances, or the fact that in a city the size of Seattle, it was the largest employer in the county. It was all those things and a thousand more, in conjunction with one another, that made it a force. U-dub punched well above its weight class.

America needs a handful of universities with the ability to pump out large numbers of skilled professionals whose parents can't afford to send them to Harvard. America needs a class of professionals who have equal skills, if not quite an equal educational pedigree. Somewhere in your city, there's a U-dub civil engineer designing the next generation of your urban infrastructure, or a U-dub medical scientist on the brink of curing some nagging human ailment. America sinks or swims on the work of such people and therefore thrives or withers with the vitality of cutting-edge public universities.

To say Ben felt out of place would be to say that the *Titanic* had encountered some minor difficulty on its maiden voyage. After Mike died, he went from being the invisible only child to the middle child in a family with only two living children. It wasn't that he thought his parents' reaction to Mike's death was wrong. Because it wasn't. They reacted the way anyone would. His mother mourned a lost child and gave birth to a new one. There's no space in that situation for a defiant teenager, none except as the typical pain in the ass that most teenagers are. Ben's dad took a couple of years to mourn and came out the other side fairly well intact. By that time, Ben was effectively grown. While it was nice to have his father back, it didn't change the fact that for years, Ben was the invisible child.

There just weren't many people like him there. He wondered whether there were people like him anywhere. The odd inner workings of his mind made him question whether he could find even five like-minded individuals on the whole of planet Earth. There weren't that many locals at U-dub. Before coming there, he'd assumed it was all locals. The students who were local all seemed to be from middle-class families, not working poor ones, some even scratching at the basement door of upper middle class. The remainder were international students and kids from rich suburbs situated just outside major urban population centers. One look at the demographics of the student body, and the prevalent Greek system at U-dub all of a sudden made sense. "Think about it. What do spoiled suburban kids like more than a kegger and fuckin' each other's girlfriends? Nothing. That's the point.

"Those places have a way of making you feel outta place in your own home. U-dub is the largest employer in King County, but if you work there—that is, if you work there but aren't faculty—you're the outsider. You could have lived in Puget Sound your whole life, worked at U-dub for decades, but eighteen-year-olds who just moved into their freshman dorm are your societal superiors. You're in their space. They stay for four years yet somehow have greater vested ownership in the place. The outsiders have immediate agency, which the locals are permanently deprived of. I guess the caste system around institutions of higher learning in America extends to places outside the Ivy League. Ha, who fuckin' would have thunk it! But there it is."

Ben was never comfortable in his body back then. Straddling two worlds, he no longer fit cleanly into the old one, and fitting into the new one was still a long way off.

He was the townie, but not even a townie in Seattle. He worked part-time at Hal of a Sub on Ninth and Pacific in downtown Tacoma. Ben laughed to himself one night as he was making someone an egg salad sub. "Fuck, I'm not even good enough to work at some shithole sandwich place near the university." Most afternoons, he'd head to the sandwich shop to work the four-to-nine shift. Most nights, he'd head home after his shift and study until one or two in the morning. Most mornings, he'd wake up early and drive to Seattle for class.

Because he couldn't be one or the other, eventually he became both without really being either. A person can't straddle two worlds forever. Eventually, a person has to become one or the other, or they have to take the virtues of both and become an entirely new thing. In time, the ability to pierce that bubble of entitlement and speak with credibility to those on high about those down below would become a great asset to him, but that was still a long way off.

During his first year at U-dub, all Ben knew was that his friends at home were beginning to speak a different language than him. They were starting to talk about apprenticeships and vocational training. They were learning how to turn the wrenches that kept civilization civil, and Ben was learning how to write essays about useless academic concepts and theories. Worse still, his friends were making money, and all Ben was doing was incurring student loan debt. The language his fellow students spoke was more foreign than the one his friends at home spoke.

With people at home, it was sad that there was an ever-widening rift between where he and they were, but at least there was a common starting point. With the people in class, there was no foundation. It was moving suddenly into something instead of being edged slowly out of something. Ben's bewilderment didn't come from a place of animosity either. In fact, to people at home, Ben was a glowing beacon of what was possible despite being from blue-collar nowhere. To his fellow students, the ones who knew where he'd come from, he was the token that illustrated what they perceived to be their own magnanimous nature. That said, until Ben figured out who he was, all the blue-collar pride of compatriots and upper-class guilt of misguided shit-heels couldn't make him feel comfortable in his own skin.

Someday he would figure out that he was the tool that neither side fully possessed, a genuine and unique thing. And it was because of this, and the fact that he was never going to fit easily into either place, that made him valuable. Back then it would have surprised Ben to learn that the people he grew up with were rooting for him because his social mobility gave them a seat at the big table of society. To those upper-class, socially insulated pretenders, he was an enigma. He could fade into their world and move freely about in the one he grew up in. He was a shade apart from both, and neither in nor out of either. Ben was a genuine go-between, and he used his talents to manipulate people in the world he had to exist in, while simultaneously opening doors for people in the world he'd originated in. It wasn't a skill that was teachable, and it wasn't something that could be purchased. It was an uncommon switch that showed up in a unique brain from time to time. It was the spark that brought the campfire to life and provided warmth to its tribe.

There were so many places that Ben was neither in nor out of, that it made more sense for him to make a home in his own mind, to view that home as a third place in between whichever poles were pushing and pulling him this way or that. There was more to it than that, but during his first year at U-dub, that was about all the sense he could make of it.

Usually when he was driving home in the afternoon, he'd talk to himself because he had no one else to talk to. He could tell Big Ben or Josh about what he was learning in class, and they'd listen, but they wouldn't really hear him. What he was learning would never matter to them. It barely mattered to Ben, and he was the one learning it. As far as talking to his fellow students, it was the rare occasion that he could talk to them even if he wanted to.

Leaving Seattle for Tacoma at two in the afternoon meant he'd barely make it back to Tacoma for his four o'clock shift at Hal of a Sub. It wasn't that Tacoma was far away, it wasn't, only about thirty miles; it's just that traffic was that bad. I-5 was the in-between place on those afternoons. Maybe, he thought, I should just live on I-5. "I mean, I must fit in there, because I-5 is nowhere, at least that in-between part of it was. Sometimes I think there should be a little hammock that exists slightly out of this dimension, just a little room that I can slide into where no one else can go except me. If I don't fit cleanly into this world, it's only fair that the universe has a little pocket dimension where only I can go."

There was no pocket dimension, but there was that in-between place in Ben's mind that he was, at that time, just beginning to adapt to living in. He didn't need much human interaction, so he just spent more and more time in there. He'd invented that place a long time ago. Really, he didn't invent it at all. It was just there, always. There wasn't a time he could remember when it wasn't there, but he'd furnished it after he discovered it, that much was true. He'd always needed it, because he'd always found a way to push himself to the periphery of any situation.

Skateboards and punk bands had pushed him to the periphery in high school. If he'd played football and listened to Korn, he'd have been right in the middle of the social scene. He'd never tried, or even desired to be in the middle of anything, but being completely pushed outside of everything, due to his misfit nature, was painful. He never knew why he did it, nor did he have any control over it, but it was a fact.

Ben's rejection of the Catholic Church as a preadolescent, for instance, left him out on an island, so to speak. Whatever the circumstance, he'd always pushed himself into the role of lone dissenting voice in a crowd of cheering group thinkers. And the outcome always remained predictably constant. So he always wound up back in that isolated place in his own mind. Sometimes Ben tried to imagine being within the group, but his mode of being was too dissimilar. He lacked the cognitive tools to even believably imagine himself in the group, so instead, he just left it alone.

As much as Ben could find a home for himself in a mental space where no one else was present or welcome, he still had to live in the actual physical world. When he was on I-5, he'd eventually wind up at Hal of a Sub, U-dub, or home. These places existed in the actual three-dimensional world. Home and Hal of a Sub was Tacoma; U-dub was Seattle. Eventually Seattle became home, at least to the extent that any place in the physical world could be home to Ben, but that was later. During his first year at U-dub, and every year prior to that, Tacoma was home. That is, Tacoma was the place in the actual world where his bed was. Even for several years after he'd moved to Seattle, Tacoma was his only physical home. "There was no in-between place in the physical world for a person stretched between Seattle and Tacoma. Maybe Federal Way, but fuck that place, right! Most of the time, home was the place in my mind where no one else was allowed. I still hope that someday I'll manage to wish my pocket dimension into being. Until then, I'm stuck here on the muddy ball with everyone else."

There were so many gaps between the two cities that no effort could be made to bridge them. The two cities were unhinged but somehow still stuck together. It was an excruciating symbiosis. To Seattle, Tacoma was like having a leg that often refused to cooperate and move in conjunction with the rest of the body. To Tacoma, Seattle was a nursery school full of whining toddlers who needed rescue from a burning building. For Seattle, it couldn't be rid of Tacoma, because even a leg that at times refused to cooperate was still better than no leg at all. For Tacoma, leaving whining toddlers to their own devices in a burning structure was unconscionable, even if you wanted to smack the shit out of every last one of those bratty little snot machines.

During his freshman year, Ben took a girl home for Thanksgiving dinner. Her name was Jennie. "Every other girl on planet Earth is named Jennifer, so kudos to her for mixing it up with her novel adaptation on an otherwise played-out name." Jennie was clearly enamored of the unique working-class perspective Ben offered in their political science course. It was the general freshman poli-sci course that everyone takes for an easy grade, and the curriculum was as broad as an ocean and as deep as a mud puddle. Jennie was from Orange County—the one in California, not Florida. "Yeah, because fuck Florida." Jennie hadn't been to Tacoma before Thanksgiving at his parents' house, and she asked Ben to compare the two cities.

"They can't be compared," he told her. "They're Athens and Sparta. Seattle is more like Portland or Vancouver BC, than it is like Tacoma. You compare Athens to, say, Rome or Carthage, not Sparta. Seattle and Tacoma are parts of one whole.

"But if you were comparing them, there's no contest, not in the context of dominance anyway. Every Tacomaite (it's Tacomaite, not Tacoman) is worth four and a half Seattleites in a rumble. If there's a brawl between Tacoma and Seattle, Tacoma beats Seattle unconscious in under a minute. If there's a knife fight between Tacoma and Seattle, Tacoma disembowels Seattle before Seattle unsheathes its knife. If there's a gun fight between Tacoma and Seattle, Seattle, for purposes of staying politically correct, will refuse to bring a gun at all. Seattle is Athens. Athens has beauty, culture, and opportunity. Tacoma is Sparta. Sparta has bleakness, cruelty, and adversity.

"Tacoma exists to protect the gleaming glass towers of the city on the hill. Seattle exists to project light in all directions from atop the highest glass tower. Tacoma and Seattle are a medieval painting of an aristocrat holding a sword in one hand and a leatherbound treatise in the other, one man with two hands. The pen and the sword. That's all they are."

Chapter 12

Her work ID card read Maria Deloera. She hated the photo. Her eyes were half-closed, probably because she wasn't ready for the guy to snap the photo. Probably, but also probably because she was only slightly less baked that first day at the city attorney's office than she was this morning. She needed it that day, and the half-asleep ID photo was the ongoing legacy of that particular foggy morning. Looking at it was a constant annoyance, but the fact that she needed it to access the office necessitated wearing it on a lanyard around her neck. Looking at it was annoying, having everyone she worked with see it all the time was embarrassing. Apparently, they don't do retakes in Chief Seattle's tribe.

She'd been at the city attorney's office for almost five years when Pete became the city attorney. It was all she'd ever done as an attorney. After leaving that cubicle drone job in 2002, she found a roommate, got a part-time job at Vivace, and went to law school as Seattle University at night. The pay was pretty good for a government job, and the cliché and obvious but still accurate thing to say was that it had great benefits. It did. Her BMW was about two years old, silver, 528xi, whatever the hell that meant. She'd gotten it new. The first couple of years there, she'd refused to get a new car. She wasn't sure she was going to stay at the city attorney's office. More to the point, she wasn't sure she was going to be able to stay.

Most of the prosecutors quit within a few months. Many of those that remained got railroaded out within a year or two by leadership through a process of toothless progressive discipline that tended to leave resignation as very desirable option. Those who couldn't cut it in a trial unit, but refused to leave, were rotated to some cake unit assignment far away from the front lines, specialty courts and the like. The handful who could cut it in a trial unit, and who still wanted to stay after realizing what the job was, lost their courage and became house cats. It was a bargain with the devil, overmatching funds to a pension, little to no copays for medical visits and procedures, flexible hours, and enough money to live on. The trade-off was that your workload kept you beholden to your computer at work, and the constant trial preparation and accompanying caseload ensured that you never went to the doctor during work hours without paying for it by working late into the evening. Maria hadn't even been to the dentist in two years. It was easier to floss really well in the morning and hope your teeth were fine than it was to take off a couple of hours in the afternoon to go to a dentist's appointment.

Every time she considered the ludicrous nature of the problem, she would wonder what to do about it. There was no solution, though. While she loathed working for the city, she knew working for a downtown law firm would be worse. The fact that her medical benefits were so great that she could get all the surgeries she wanted seemed like an upside-down rationalization to stay in a job that was objectively terrible. The city allowed employees to roll over as much sick time as they wanted. That made sense to Maria, since she was always so underwater with work that she never used any sick time. Maria had almost eight weeks accrued. On the rare occasion she took a sick day, she typically ended up working at home anyway.

"Ha, if I ever get sick enough to take advantage of my Cadillac benefits, all I have to do is use some of the hundreds of hours of sick time I've accrued and work until eleven at night while I recover from surgery. What a bargain!"

She was thinking out loud.

Actually, she was talking to herself, but she didn't care to frame it like that. Thinking out loud sounded better. She was a trial prosecutor, a storyteller, and stories were all about the framing.

A couple of years ago she stopped wrestling with reality. She stopped caring about whether she would win or lose this trial or that. She stopped worrying about whether she would be gently persuaded to resign by her superiors. Once she settled into the job and stopped giving a fuck about the outcomes of her behavior, she finally fit in. She gave a fuck, but more so about the battered women she saw every day, never about the office, the court, or white-bread slimeball defense attorneys. Apathy, security, and monotony were the pillars holding up government jobs, and the city attorney's office was a prime example.

The BMW was nice, only a couple of years old. The apartment was nice, only a little too close to a very loud gay bar on Capitol Hill. The clothes were nice, only slightly less expensive than the very expensive ones. Someone had once told her that more education equals more freedom, a professional degree ensures security, and lawyers are rich. In fact, this was all bullshit. Most lawyers aren't rich. Because they worked so many hours, Maria doubted that many of them made much more than minimum wage. A professional degree only secures a different kind of security—the ability to be middle class in the big city instead of the sticks. More education never equaled more freedom. Student loan debt ensured that most people with multiple years of higher education were more hemmed into servitude than her parents and grandparents ever were.

When her '81 Corolla finally died, she knew she wasn't going anywhere. She was trapped in a professional cell of her own making, shackled by golden handcuffs. Her devil's bargain was complete. She wore the golden handcuffs. To celebrate this acceptance of ultimate failure, she got a brand-new BMW. She'd leased it, which seemed like a glorified version of renting to own your furniture. Immediately an image from last Thanksgiving popped into her head of her mom frantically scrubbing red wine out of a couch cushion. Maria had gotten a little tipsy, and her wine splashed onto the couch. Through her mother's eyes, it happened in slow motion. Maria couldn't help but laugh.

It wasn't humorous; it was ludicrous, like most things. Maria's mom had been paying for that couch since Maria was in high school, and she still didn't own it. Maria hated that couch and considered hauling it out to the yard and lighting it on fire. Freeing her mother from that couch would do her good, Maria smugly thought to herself. Right about then, she knocked over her pipe. Ash and hot coals fell onto the leather passenger seat. She frantically tried to stamp it out with the palm of her hand. She then scrubbed at it with a Wet-Nap from the pack she kept in her purse.

"At least my stained rented pile of shit has a sharp silver paint job and leather seats. Maybe I can haul it out to the yard and set it on fire. But I don't have a yard because I live in an apartment in the city. Oh well."

She was thinking out loud again, not talking to herself, thinking out loud.

Right about then, that new white boy from the office appeared, wearing his cleanly pressed white-boy suit, and not shockingly a white shirt. She was used to white boys. Her band had been full of white boys. Seattle was full of white boys. College and law school had definitely been full of white boys. The DPD was full of Ivy League white boys, the second worst kind of white boy next to the frat bro white boy. The city attorney's office was full of white boys too, like her supervisor, Alan Thorpe. Now the city attorney's office had another white boy, which in her opinion meant the city attorney's office wasn't just full of white boys but overfull.

He walked up to the BMW with that typical white-boy swagger. He knocked on her window. She rolled it down, and a cloud of pot smoke hit him square in the face.

"Did you bring enough for the whole class?"

He paused for a minute, listening. "Hey, is that Jawbreaker?"

"All right, maybe you're okay—for a white boy," she said.

<h1 align="center">Chapter 13</h1>

A couple of months later, Ben was sitting at the counsel table in Courtroom 1002 at SMC. Because the city attorney's office didn't do any of the felony prosecutions, SMC was effectively the perpetual farm team, triple-A ball exclusively. The only courtrooms at SMC with any natural light were the ones on the end of the building. Courtroom 1002 was sandwiched in the middle and thus was one of the courtrooms with no windows. These courtrooms seemed extra dark too. It was as if they artificially lowered the lights to make the courtrooms seem more sinister. Ben felt like he was sitting in a courtroom in one of the Christopher Nolan *Batman* movies.

He wondered why the aesthetic of every courtroom was wall-to-wall paneled wood. The SMC courtrooms were more "American gothic" in their appeal, whereas down the road at King County Superior Court, the courtrooms had more of a "frontier justice" mood to them. "Just once, I'd like to see a mod style courtroom. The judge's chair could be one of those swiveling ball chairs with lime-green cushions. The counsel tables could be walnut with decorative horizontal slats, and they could hang a print of Andy Warhol's Elizabeth Taylor portrait. The defense could show up to court on Vespas, and the prosecutors on Triumphs. What a world that could be, mods and rockers duking it out in the wettest of Pete Townsend's wet dreams."

As TDA supervisor for SMC, Tim was TDA's great white hope that day. Ben figured Tim stuck around SMC, instead of rotating to a superior court assignment, because he was a bully and got off on beating up the new city prosecutors. In superior court, the defense didn't have the same unfair advantage. The jury pools came from the whole of King County and, as such, were more conservative and therefore friendlier to the government. Over there, the judges were professionals who were more interested in making good law than they were in carrying this or that side's water. Those superior court judges took their responsibilities seriously. At SMC, prison abolitionists stood at the door and handed jury nullification pamphlets to every potential juror who arrived. Most of the judges were actively out to get the prosecutors. And the jury pool was composed of rich, educated Seattleites carrying around about three tons of white guilt apiece. They were apathetic toward the government at best, and openly hostile at worst. And of course, the DPD attorneys were well armed and prepared to take down any city prosecutor that survived all those obstacles. SMC was kangaroo court, and Tim was the silverback gorilla and self-appointed guardian of the accused in Seattle.

Tim credited himself as being quite clever. He called the city prosecutors G-men, and he called the new prosecutors junior G-men. He was big, too, like about six four, not really built but big. He'd adopted the public defender uniform—that is, tweed sports jacket, gingham-patterned button-down shirt, denim slacks, cheap polyester tie, and brown Dockers brand oxfords. This universally accepted public defender uniform is professional camouflage nearly as convincing as Ben's own, but only to the untrained eye.

"Tim went to Harvard Law School. Dressing like a community college English professor was only level one of his deception." The shit-eating grin he wore only thinly veiled the silver spoon in his mouth. Unfortunately for everyone, from time-to-time Tim saw fit to open his mouth and speak. Fortunately for everyone, when he did, they got a peek at that baked-in rich boy entitlement. As convincing as his uniform could be, there was no professional camouflage for his vernacular, and that day, when he stood up to do his voir dire, everyone in the jury venire started seething with resentment. It was certainly the case that people in Seattle almost always acquitted defendants of misdemeanor crimes, mainly because that was part and parcel of the Seattle DNA, but that didn't mean they liked being talked down to by grotesquely tall wads of Ivy League–brand white bread dough.

At the morning recess, Ben was standing at the urinal unloading the half a pot of coffee he'd drank that morning. Tim walked up to the urinal next to him. Ben wasn't short. In fact, he was somewhat tall, but he immediately felt Tim looming over him, using his odd height to try to intimidate him. Ben always preferred fighting guys who were taller than him. "It's because their balls are right at perfect gut-punch height. Most people will cover their face when they're fighting, some will cover their stomachs, but nobody cups their balls to protect them. If their balls are at punching height, I punch 'em in the balls. Tall guys should protect their balls, not their heads. Who's going to punch some eight-foot-tall guy in the face. Use your brains tall guys. Seriously."

"What do you think you're going to do in there, junior G-man? I don't know why you prosecutors even bother showing up to trials here. You never win. You're certainly not going to win this one."

"I don't have to win, Tim. All I have to do is give you a bloody nose. Once people see you bleed, your aura of invincibility fades away."

Ben turned toward Tim, cock out, midstream. Piss shot onto Tim's pantleg and splashed up from the tile floor where it cascaded over those ugly-ass oxfords that encapsulated Tim's entitled little feet.

"Are you fucking crazy? What the fuck's the matter with you!"

"What the fuck's the matter with you, Harvard? You're the one with piss all over your shoes!"

Ben glanced up at Tim's frightened eyes. Right then, Tim could have been ten feet tall and wide as a refrigerator and it wouldn't have mattered. Ben knew something that most people didn't. Dominance doesn't belong to the loudest ape. It belongs to the ape with the fortitude to piss on the loudest ape.

Tim didn't hang around to wash his hands. He didn't even bother to wipe off his shoes with a paper towel. He backed up and nearly fell over the garbage can by the door. Ben never flushed public urinals, and he never washed his hands after he pissed. "Why fuckin' bother? All I ever touch in there is my own cock, and I like the way it smells on my hands. It's the aromatic scent of me. I'd brew it into a tea if I could." After Ben zipped up, he grabbed a paper towel out of the wall dispenser, opened the door with it, and pitched the paper towel onto the restroom floor. Just because he didn't wash his hands didn't mean he liked touching filthy door handles.

Ben had a rapport with people, and even though he'd never done a voir dire before, he was charming and likable. Everybody knew that jurors made up their mind during jury selection. The only point of the trial was to give jurors something that they could use to justify their predetermined outcome. It was a popularity contest that defense attorneys didn't even have to be popular to win. They just had to be on the politically popular side of the ideological spectrum. In fact, they could be patently unlikable and still win the trial, and they normally did.

The prosecutor has to be likable as a person to sway the jury during jury selection because the prosecutor is advocating for the politically unpopular position. That is, conviction. The defense attorney, even pompous ones like Tim, were advocating for the prevailing politically popular position. That is, acquit no matter what.

Ben didn't win that trial, but he didn't lose it either. It was a hung jury, but a hung jury on a misdemeanor assault in SMC was a victory of sorts for a prosecutor. For the first time in his life, Ben recognized how being in between worlds could be useful.

A jury venire is a cross section of the population. How does one speak to the socioeconomically unfortunate in the venire without pissing off the rich fuckers, and vice versa? Most people, including most trial lawyers, never figure it out. Tim certainly never did. He just went on winning cases by parroting what most Seattleites wanted to hear. He probably even thought he was likable, since he kept winning. He likely never understood that he won because he was preaching to the choir. That day, Ben figured something out, one little piece of the puzzle that would one day expand into a clear picture of his existence and purpose. He figured out that communicating with people wasn't something that you could learn how to do. If it was, Tim would have mastered it long ago. No, communicating with people was a gift, definitely something that a person could get better at, but a gift you were born with nonetheless.

Back then, there was a ritual at SMC. The newer attorneys at the various public defender divisions in Seattle would come down to SMC anytime there was a trial. They'd come to gawk at the prosecutor the way people gawk at the animals in a zoo. They'd come to take notes. Most importantly, they'd come to watch the city prosecutors eat a slice of humble pie after being trounced by Tim. Typically, the writing was on the wall by the time the prosecutor called their first witness. But that trial had a different tone. The public defenders in the gallery could see it as well. There was a scent in the air. It was fear and desperation, and perhaps a little urine as well. Nobody could remember the last time that a public defender in trial at SMC had seemed unsure about the outcome.

The defense would lose trials from time to time, but those were always aberrations. The occasional loss could always be chalked up to something like overwhelming evidence that even a Seattle jury couldn't ignore. The trial that week was different. It was different because a prosecutor had figured out a way to break through the noise. Ben was starting to figure out the code he had to break in order to win. Ben was able to convince some members of a Seattle jury that they should care that somebody got punched by some random stranger. Defense didn't sweat much about losing a couple of trials where overwhelming evidence made guilt irrefutable, but a prosecutor who could sway opinion with nothing more than a charming demeanor and persuasive rational inferences was a serious problem for them.

A hung jury wasn't an acquittal, but usually it was just as good as one, since the city rarely retried the defendant after a hung jury. Usually, it was cause for an end-of-week happy hour where the defense attorneys could slap each other on the back about how righteously great they all were.

That week, a few wondered how the victim who got punched felt. A few wondered why Tim wasn't his normal boisterous self. More than a few wondered how an upstart provincial townie had taken the reigning champion of SMC twelve rounds. The remainder wondered if they were witnessing the beginning of the end of a golden age for public defenders in Seattle. They had their happy hour that week, but it was a fairly morose affair.

Erin O'Connell was there that evening. Erin had been in the courtroom gallery for most of the week, not that anyone had taken any notice. But at that Friday evening happy hour, a couple of her colleagues noticed that Erin seemed cheerier than usual, certainly cheerier than the rest of them. Three or four of them even thought that Erin seemed downright giddy. None of them guessed why. She didn't say it out loud. She barely even allowed herself to think it, but to her, that Friday had been the best day at work that she could remember having in years.

Chapter 14

As one might expect, in any given life, many eventless months will come and go. In Ben's 2010, this had certainly become the pattern. He settled into the job, and even learned how to be fairly good at it. Most of it was negotiating plea deals and going to the multitude of pretrial hearings that is an integral part of being a prosecutor in a busy city attorney's office. By November, none of the DPD attorneys had challenged Ben to a metaphorical or actual pissing contest, and Tim, who had been scarce since their trial, had not challenged Ben to a rematch.

It made no difference to Ben. He knew Tim wouldn't do anything. "What on earth could he possibly do? Is he gonna call the Seattle Police Department's non-emergency line and say, 'I'm a public defender, and this prosecutor peed on my shoes several months ago'?" No, Tim couldn't do that. He may have warned a few of his confederates to steer clear of Ben, but broadcasting the incident to a wide audience would only serve to make him look flaccid. Besides, any cop taking that report would piss themselves laughing while writing it. Also, as a criminal defense attorney, Tim knew it was an unprovable case.

In an odd way, Ben had hoped Tim would do something.

Technically, peeing on Tim's shoes was a misdemeanor assault. Ben was delighted by the idea that if Tim had wanted to report it, he'd have been reliant on a Seattle cop to take the report, and reliant on a prosecutor from Ben's office to prosecute the case. Tim spent his working life explaining away similar transgressions on the part of his clients as inconsequential, not a public safety concern, and not worthy of wasting the criminal justice system's time. Ben wondered how inconsequential such events seemed to Tim after he had to throw out his pee-soaked shoes.

Similarly, it appeared that the male DPD attorneys had some safety concerns, because not one of them would step into the restroom when Ben was around. Every area of the courthouse had cameras on it, but the restrooms were black boxes. Everybody knew people went in there to pee, but nobody outside could ever know for sure where the pee went. Ben could actually see some of the male DPD attorneys squirm during recesses, trying to hold back the contents of their coffee-saturated bladders when Ben was around.

Of some note, Ben had been fucking Erin O'Connell for about six months. To Ben, she was an interesting woman. Erin had blond hair and big breasts, but she pinned her hair into a bun and kept her breasts hidden under cleverly tailored blazers. She also wore glasses, glasses that Ben was pretty sure she didn't really need. She always wore makeup, but it was the kind of makeup designed to make a person's face look plainer, no dark lipliner or loud eye makeup.

Sometime in early June—Ben couldn't really remember the specific date—Erin cornered him in the courthouse elevator. It was the first time he'd noticed her breasts, likely because it was the first time he'd ever seen her with the top two buttons of her white button-down shirt undone. It was Friday, and she seemed sort of sloppy drunk, so Ben assumed that the DPD happy hour had started a little early for Erin. When the elevator got to the lobby, Erin sauntered out, expecting Ben to be following behind. When she turned to see if Ben was looking at her, he wasn't. He hadn't gotten out of the elevator. Instead, he hit the button for the tenth floor. Through the closing doors, Ben said, "I forgot my phone upstairs. Later."

When that Monday rolled around, Erin became more deliberate. Ben was finishing his morning pretrial calendar, and Erin was lying in wait in the hallway outside Courtroom 1103.

"Let's go get some lunch," she said.

"I never eat lunch," Ben replied.

"Then watch me eat. Come on, I'm hungry."

They didn't actually get lunch that day. Erin was attractive, but good Irish Catholic Republican militants don't fuck evil Protestant loyalist militants who lived across the bog. She was looking at him and preening again. Ben figured the quickest way to kill whatever this was in its cradle was to say something inappropriate and offensive.

"I'm not wasting my afternoon on lunch. If you want to waste my afternoon, it's gonna be at my place."

Erin looked up at him with her big doe eyes and spoke quietly, her full, pouty lips forming the words. "I'll drive."

That had been a good afternoon, but she'd been sleeping over a lot since then. It wasn't that Ben didn't like girls, and it wasn't that Erin wasn't attractive. It was just that Ben mostly liked being on his own, and someone being around all the time seriously cut into the time he liked to spend playing *Halo*. He also didn't like sharing his bed, but she kept staying so late after they had sex, she'd just sort of invite herself to stay the night.

Ben spent a lot of nights that summer sleeping on his couch, because, most nights, he'd wait for her to fall asleep in his bed, and then he'd move to the living room and play *Halo* until three in the morning. Things kept being left at his place as well. "Said another way, Erin kept bringing girl crap over to my apartment and leaving it all over the fuckin' place."

By November, Erin was under the impression that they were in an exclusive relationship. It was mostly exclusive, but that had more to do with the fact that Ben didn't like wasting his free time conning women into sleeping with him. He preferred call girls, and the Internet had streamlined transactional sex into one-stop shopping. He'd only had a few over to his place since June, mostly on account of Erin always being underfoot. In any case, Erin was mostly right about the exclusivity of their relationship. In other words, Ben wasn't dating anyone else. "Call girls yankin' your crank for cash doesn't really count, you know."

It was November, and Ben loved Thanksgiving. The Sunday before, he was sitting in his living room watching a PBS documentary about the Troubles. He wanted to nap in his bed, but Erin was in there reading a book. They were talking about Derry on the documentary. The Brits renamed it Londonderry way back when.

"Those fuckin' WASP loyalist motherfuckers got some fuckin' nerve. They think they own every-fuckin'-thing."

"I can't hear you, babe. What'd you say?"

Ben glanced down the hall. From his couch, he could see she'd propped herself up on his pillows into a sitting position to read. There she was, like always, occupying his room like she owned it.

"This fuckin' WASP loyalist motherfucker got some fuckin'

nerve. She thinks she owns every-fuckin'-thing."

"Babe, come in here and tell me. I can't hear you all the way in there."

Ben wasn't talking to her, even if he was talking about her.

"Never-fuckin'-mind," he shouted down the hall at her.

Big Ben called on the phone, and Ben talked to his dad for about fifteen minutes about the plan for Thanksgiving.

After Ben hung up, Erin came out to the living room and said, "What time are you leaving on Thursday?"

Ben was actually thinking of heading to Tacoma Wednesday after work, but instead he told Erin, "I don't know. Probably after I get up on Thursday. What are you doing on Thanksgiving?"

"Well, my family is in Massachusetts, and I have too much work to just up and leave over the holiday weekend."

Ben pretended to think out loud. "Hmm. There're so many people from your office from out of state, I'm sure they're having some sort of get-together. They probably all buy a bunch of liquor and get wasted at somebody's place. That would probably be fun. Maybe?"

"Is that something you'd want to go to?"

"What? No! Why would I spend my Thanksgiving with those fuckin' assholes? Besides, you just heard me talking to my dad about going to my parents' house."

"So, did you want me to stay over here Wednesday night and bring some extra clothes with me?

"You mean like a coat? Is it supposed to be cold on Thursday? I don't fuckin' know. It's never that cold around here, so I never really wear a coat."

"The extra clothes would be so that I have something to wear to Thanksgiving dinner."

"If you want to bring extra clothes with you, that's your business. You don't really ever ask if you can stay over any other time, and half of your wardrobe is already strangling my poor closet, so I'm not sure why you're asking now."

"I don't know, Ben. I guess that if I'm going to meet your family, it might be nice to have something clean to wear."

"What?"

The thought that she was angling for an invitation had genuinely not occurred to Ben.

"So, you want to go to Tacoma with me?"

"Yeah! Dummy! Where else would I be on Thanksgiving?"

"Maybe, like, with your friends at work, or your family in Massachusetts."

"Do you want to come to Massachusetts with me?"

"Fuck no! That sounds fuckin' terrible."

"What's that supposed to mean?"

"Don't you think that would be a little awkward, me meeting your family?"

"Why?"

"Because my dad is an electrician. Because my dead brother was a crack addict. Because I grew up in the most stereotypical white-trash, working-poor neighborhood imaginable. Because I went to a state school. What do you think, me and your dad are going to sit and watch the Apple Cup? Get fuckin' real! Grow up! Grow a fuckin' brain! Why would your parents want to meet me?"

"Maybe because I've been telling them about you for months."

"Why would you fuckin' do that?"

"Because I want them to know that I'm in a meaningful, committed relationship."

"But you're not!"

"Then what are we doing here?"

"I have no idea what we're doing here, but just because you're always hanging around doesn't make this a relationship."

"This isn't a relationship. So I'm supposed to believe that your parents don't want to meet the woman you practically live with?"

"I doubt it!"

"Why?"

"There are a lot of people my parents don't know exist who they wouldn't necessarily want to meet."

"They don't know you have a girlfriend?"

"Nope. Because I don't have a girlfriend. And to be honest, even if you were my girlfriend, I doubt I would call them up and tell them about you."

"Wait, what? Why?"

"I don't know. I just don't do that. What do you think people like my parents would have to say to someone like you?"

"What's that supposed to mean?"

"We fuckin' hate people like you. We tack pictures of people like you up on dartboards at the corner bar. My ancestors burned effigies of people like you in the town square. I don't tell my friends about you either."

"What! What about your friend Jason at work?"

"I was talking about my other friends, but no, I definitely don't tell people at work about you either. Why would I do that?"

"Why not, we all work together."

"No we don't, people at my office hate you more than my parent's would. Do you really think I'm going to tell an office full of union member municipal prosecutors about the Ivy League public defender I'm bangin'? I think there's actually a dartboard at my office with Tim's face tacked to it. I mean, why would you tell people at your office that you're fuckin' me?"

"I have. I've told them all, lots of times. I have a picture of you and me on my desk."

"Really? When did you and I take a picture together?"

"You're a fucking prick! And it's a selfie I took of us at the Dick's on Capitol Hill."

"Yeah, I remember the cheeseburgers that night. Dick's is pretty good, especially after a few beers. It's the milkshakes too, you know."

"Prick! Prick, prick, prick!"

"All right, I'm a prick. So, I'm gonna take off."

"This is your apartment."

"Yeah, but it's been a while since it really felt like my apartment. I've actually been spending a lot of time just sort of hanging out in my Barracuda lately."

"You sit in your car?"

"Yeah, you know, the app store is starting to get some pretty good games for your phone, so I've been doing that a lot. You can kind of sit anywhere and play games as long as your battery holds out, and I got a cord that charges my iPhone off the cigarette lighter. I got a pillow and a sleeping bag down there too, CDs to listen to as well. It's pretty cozy. I put a sixer of Rainier tall boys in a cooler in the trunk, and there's some chips in the back seat."

Erin started pacing back and forth on the living room rug, hand on forehead, talking to herself. "I cannot believe this! It's like we're from different planets. This isn't how people are supposed to act. This isn't how normal people act. What is the matter with this guy?"

"So, like I said, I'm gonna to take off."

"I'm going to your parents' house on Thanksgiving."

"Don't you think that would be a little awkward?"

"I can put up with a little awkwardness. Don't worry about me."

"I'm not. I meant it would be a little awkward for the rest of us."

"I'm coming to Thanksgiving with you!"

"So, I'm gonna to take off now, alright."

"I'm coming to Thanksgiving."

Ben wanted the last word, but not as bad as Erin did, so he bit his tongue as he moved toward the door.

Chapter 15

en slept in the Barracuda that night. When he went up to his place in the morning, Erin was gone, so he grabbed a shower and put on his clean suit and shirt. He got his buddy Jason to cover his pretrials Monday afternoon. He had no appearances in court on Tuesday or Wednesday. He was planning on leaving straight from work on Wednesday for his parents' place. Up in SMT, he felt fairly well insulated from the outside. You couldn't get onto the fifty-third floor without a badge, so he was pretty sure he wasn't going to run into Erin. He'd let his cell phone battery go dead, so he had plausible deniability about not returning her calls and texts. "I can't very well answer a phone when I lost it and the battery's gone dead, you know."

Ben liked Erin. He actually really liked her. "Outta all those preachy Ivy League carpetbaggin' pieces of shit over there at the DPD, she was the best of them. I always thought she must have been switched at birth, because not one of those self-righteous windbags ever picked up on how fucked up them being here was.

"The DPD never hired people from around here. I went to school with tons of people from Seattle who wanted to be public defenders. Not me, I never fuckin' wanted to work there, but some of the people I went to school with did. The DPD wouldn't even interview them most of the time. Refusing to hire people from around here and then going out and hiring rich white kids from the other side of the country was a slap in the face to the community. Worst of all, those rich kids didn't even need the paycheck. The DPD literally paid rich kids money they didn't need while denying lawyers from the community, who did need the income, any opportunity to represent criminal defendants."

Erin was the only one of them who ever recognized that she was carrying around five generations of blue-blooded white guilt. Pushing her way into a job that was better suited to people from the socioeconomically disadvantaged communities that most criminal defendants came from wasn't to help them. It was to help herself. It was do-gooderism born of guilt. The indigent and accused of Seattle didn't need Erin's confession or penance. Erin needed it. She got it by stealing a job in a place she wasn't wanted, representing people who despised her. The world didn't need her penance either. As with most things in life, what appeared to be altruistic on the surface was nothing more than a paltry attempt to wash clean a guilty conscience. Erin recognized that the best thing she could have done for the downtrodden was to simply stay in her lane. Attempting to do social mobility in reverse just continued to disadvantage and displace those below her, and in the most ironic way imaginable, she'd continued to perpetuate the cycle of domination that her lineage had been guilty of all these generations.

Ben liked Erin because she was self-aware. He liked that she had the courage to stare at the boogeyman of her existence and accept the ludicrous irony of it all. She was the best version of what she could be. Her ability to focus on one singular point on the horizon and move toward it helped her to become the only self-aware DPD do-gooder Ben had ever met.

At that very moment, it was precisely that singular focus that was driving Erin to locate and trap Ben on that Wednesday afternoon. Erin was stubborn but focused. Ben was sloppy but clever. Erin also thought Ben was charming in a neo-roguish sort of way. His cell kept going straight to voicemail. She'd stopped by his apartment more than once in the early part of the week, but Ben was good at slipping by her. She'd be watching his apartment building's secure front door, waiting for her chance to confront him. Then she'd look up at his living room window, and he'd be standing there.

That ghastly muscle car he drove would always magically appear, parked on Harrison Street where he always parked. She couldn't stand that thing. Whenever she was sitting in it, all she could hear was that loud fume-spewing motor, worn-out springs squeaking in the seat, and that music. It smelled like spent gasoline inside. But the music, she thought, the music was always up way too loud, just racket, not really music at all. Punk rock, she rolled her eyes even though no one was there to appreciate it, whatever that meant. She was thinking about the first time he drove her home. That idiot never wore his seatbelt either, she thought, even on the interstate. Erin never felt safe in that steel trap, even with her seatbelt on. It always jerked forward when Ben shifted it into a higher gear. It was built when cars were essentially just rolling coffins. Be that as it may, she still managed to somehow not to hear it creep up and park on Harrison. She started wondering if Ben had installed some secret silent mode in his car.

On Monday evening, she buzzed his apartment. No answer. While she was standing there, she started to realize that he never answered his buzzer. She was beginning to think it didn't even work. That would figure. That building was the sort of building that nobody ever bothered to fix up. She walked around the building to discover that he'd turned out the living room light even though she'd seen it on a few minutes before. On Tuesday evening, she parked right in front of his apartment building's secure front door. She figured there was no way for him to slip past her if she was six feet away from the door, but he did. She saw that car of his, saw the living room light, and buzzed. No answer.

"She didn't know that I had found the super's key ring a few months back. I called him up and gave him the key ring back, but not before I ran over to the QFC and copied a few of the more important keys on that ring. Paramount among them, the key to the service entrance around back. Also, I'd snipped the line to the door buzzer in my apartment when I moved in. I hate that fuckin' thing. Neighbors buzz you when they forgot their keys. Random weirdos buzz all the apartments for shits and giggles. Angry ex-girlfriends are an omnipresent hazard, so you don't want to give them another way to get ahold of you. Why would anyone want people on the street to have a direct line to your inner sanctum! If you want to get ahold of me, just yell up to my apartment window like a normal person."

By Wednesday, Erin wasn't fucking around anymore. She left work an hour early, drove her black Mercedes into the SMT parking lot, backed into the stall next to Ben's car, and waited. The way she'd backed in was driver's side to driver's side. She was so close that there was no way to open the driver's-side doors of either vehicle.

Ben really was clever, but he was sloppy. Most of his slickest moves were actually just on-the-fly innovations. He moved through life quickly, and he missed a lot of details. His written work, while well thought out, could be riddled with typos and obvious errors. His failure to anticipate fairly expected tactics by opposing lawyers left him scrambling on the record more than once.

Ben's brain didn't work correctly until he was threatened in some way, but once threatened, the most genius work-arounds presented themselves to him. This phenomenon garnered him a reputation at work. People always thought his folksy vernacular was just a put-on. They thought his supposed blind spots—missing obvious legal maneuverings from opposing attorneys—was just him baiting a trap that he would spring at the right moment. Nobody thought that someone could be so absent minded when given all the time in the world to prepare, but so brilliant when cornered.

Ben did plan, and he hated that he seemed cursed to miss fairly blatant obstacles sitting in plain sight. But he loved the fact that he was able to pivot in real time. Many times, in the coming years he'd be performing a direct examination during trial and he'd hear a witness say something a certain way, something he wasn't expecting, and he'd look over and see that the jury had heard it the same way. He'd literally depart from his written questions altogether and follow the line of questioning to wherever it led. Often, he'd start a closing argument, referring to his notes, then pivot mid-sentence and take the whole thing in another direction.

Ben had a read on people that never failed him, and a situational awareness that gave him a five-second head start on everyone else. He'd swerve to avoid a car crash that nobody knew was imminent. He'd move out of the way of objects coming at him that weren't even in transit yet. He'd spot the overarching weak point in someone's argument before they finished their first point.

"Planning is important. I wish I was better at it, but I'm sort of shit at it if I'm being honest. Pivoting is more important. No matter how good your plan is, you're going to have to pivot. No matter how shit your plan is, you're going to have to pivot. If you're thrown unexpectedly into a situation that nobody could have reasonably planned for, you're going to have to pivot. A smart man once wrote, 'The best laid schemes o' Mice an' Men Gang aft agley.' More recently, an even smarter man said, 'Everybody has a plan until they get punched in the face.' My brain operates in two-wheel drive most of the time, and two-wheel drive is more than sufficient for most occasions. Jeopardy always flipped the four-wheel drive switch in my brain. It hooked the bumper winch to the tree stump and pulled until the fuckin' thing popped outta the ground."

That Wednesday afternoon, Ben had missed a pretty obvious sign like usual. He'd been dodging Erin for almost three days. He'd seen her car at his apartment building both Monday and Tuesday after work. Both evenings, he was able to park without her noticing pretty easily. Both evenings, he pretty easily slipped in through the service entrance around back. His phone was dead in his bag, and the door buzzer had been dead since he killed it on move-in day. He didn't go straight to bed either night, but he killed the lights almost immediately.

Ben doubted that Erin would be skulking around his building for a third day in a row, so he started thinking again about packing a bag and heading to his parents' house that night. His floor at work was key-card access only, so he knew she wouldn't be surprising him there either, but he didn't think about the SMT parking lot.

Ben left the office that afternoon, descending the great vein of the gigantic penis. When he reached the lobby, the little tacky lobby, Ben gave it a once-over. If Erin was going to be somewhere, the little tacky lobby, he thought, would likely be the place. He made his way through the other lobby, the big tacky lobby, to the bank of elevators that went to the parking structure. Maria Deloera from his office was standing there, waiting.

It was always awkward, Ben thought. "It must be, isn't it awkward for everyone?" Ben could connect with people without effort. He couldn't understand how, because he genuinely found most human interactions to be uncomfortable and unwanted. He chalked it up to his brain's four-wheel drive. "Awkward small talk with a coworker is all about posturing. It's strategy. It's adversarial. Every human interaction is essentially conflict. Sometimes it's good-natured debate, but it's always a metaphorical brawl for dominance. Who moves first? Is making the first move cool, or is it desperate? Is waiting silently stoic, or is it creepy?" Maria broke the awkward silence.

"Plans for Thanksgiving?"

"Just gonna go down to my parents' place in Tacoma. You?"

"Yeah, family stuff, you know how it is."

The elevator arrived. Ben hit P2. Maria hit P3. It was one of those little steel coffin elevators, not like the nice ones you see in beautiful buildings. Ben and Maria were used to being shoved into these little steel coffins with other people. The elevators at SMC were very similar. They weren't used to being shoved into these little steel coffins with each other. In fact, other than that time Ben saw her getting baked in the parking garage, and the gossip scoop on Ben's first day (the extent of Maria's efforts at peer mentoring), they hadn't interacted much at all.

The coffin lid slid open on P2. Ben started walking.

"See you after the holiday," he said.

"See ya," she replied.

He didn't make it very far. He'd taken only two steps out of the elevator before the four-wheel drive kicked in. There weren't many cars left on P2 the afternoon before Thanksgiving. Ben could see the unmistakable front end of the Barracuda from his vantage point, but the rest of his car was being blocked by another. It was black and shiny, cold and hard. It was like Darth Vader popping unexpectedly out of the jungle on Dagoba. That steel hood ornament, the three-pointed star of the Mercedes-Benz company unmistakable.

Ben locked eyes with Erin. She was wearing a high-buttoned black blazer with a starched white button-down shirt. Her blond hair was up in a twisty bun. She looked like a Gestapo officer, and Ben started hearing German shepherds barking in the background. He saw her leaping from the driver's seat, shouting orders in deliberately abrupt German syllables. She was pointing a Walther at him, a P38, a Luger maybe, he couldn't tell for sure.

It wasn't a hallucination because it only happened in his head, not in his eyes. It always happened like that. It took half a second for his brain to characterize an event as dangerous, and to do so in overly theatrical detail. Erin really did leap out of her car, but for some reason unbeknownst to Ben, she climbed over center console and popped out the passenger side. Ben's four-wheel drive brain buckled Ben's knees without asking him for permission to do so. Now he was three feet tall. That got him below the eyeline of the cars, but he knew that wouldn't confuse Erin for long. Ben didn't underestimate Erin. He assumed her huntress instincts were likely as keen as his prey instincts were.

For a second, the sharp pain that stabs through the heart when a person is startled kept his from beating at all. That was a second ago. Now it throbbed against the inside of his rib cage. "Beads of sweat form on your brow in less than a second. How is that even possible? No time for that." His field of vision narrowed, but what he could see, he saw in great detail.

He heard the elevator door start to close behind him. The little steel coffin had become a lifeboat. He spun 180 degrees and duckwalked in his Prada's to the elevator door while Erin goose-stepped toward him in her jackboots. He'd taken two steps out of the elevator, but now with the duckwalking, it took him five steps to get back; meanwhile, Erin's blitzkrieg death march eroded the space between them with frightening speed.

The elevator door was one of those shitty ones that opened and closed from one side instead of two doors opening in the center, so Ben had to dive for the still open right side and slither through like a snake. He was in the lifeboat. Unfortunately, in order to keep elevator doors from crushing people, there's a sensor that opens the door again when someone squirms through, as Ben had just done.

Ben scrambled to his feet. Maria was staring at him with puzzled amusement. In fact, she looked as if it was the funniest thing she'd seen all week.

Gestapo Erin was bearing down on them.

"Push the button! Push the fuckin' button!" Ben muttered to Maria through clenched teeth.

Maria was openly laughing by that point.

As the elevator door closed, Ben looked at Erin and said, "See you Friday, babe."

Clearly Maria wasn't sure what the etiquette was in this sort of situation, so she just kept giggling and directed a fingers-waggling wave toward Erin as the little steel coffin's door finally, and mercifully, sealed her and Ben inside.

Ten seconds after the elevator door had opened to reveal the situation he'd failed to plan for, Ben was safely traveling to P3 with Maria. He was safe for the moment, but he wouldn't be safe for long. Erin could see where the elevator was traveling, and it wouldn't take her long to make her way to the stairs. She was an extremely smart and motivated girl. From there, she'd be on top of him again in less than a minute. She was fast too, probably from all the tennis, and with how slow the elevators were at SMT, he genuinely feared she'd be waiting outside the elevator when it arrived on P3.

"What the fuck was that all about, white boy?"

"Nothing. What? Why? Why do you ask? My car isn't up there. It must be down here."

"And the ducking and diving into the elevator?"

"You know how long it takes for the elevator to come back once the door closes. Who needs that? You gotta seize the day. Carpe diem and all that, you know."

"And what about Erin O'Connell, looking like the Terminator, closing in on you like you're Sarah Connor?"

"Hey, man, whatever. That's how I roll. She can get the next elevator. We don't need to wait around for her. I hate when people are like 'Hold it for me, please!' and they're like way across the other side of the parking lot. Man, you're either here when the door closes, or you're not. I'm not sittin' waitin' on that nonsense. And I really got more of a Nazi vibe from her than Terminator."

The door opened on P3. Ben peeked around quickly. Erin wasn't there. Yet.

"Where's your car, white boy?"

"I must have, like, taken the bus or something. Fuck me. I mean, I'd forget my head if it wasn't attached, you know, Hey, whatever. You feel like dropping me off somewhere? Anywhere?"

"Yeah, okay."

They were walking in tandem past the empty parking stalls on P3.

"Where do you live?"

"Capitol Hill."

The telltale chirp of a key fob opening her BMW's doors echoed across the steel and concrete of the empty parking structure.

"Get in."

A second after sitting down in Maria's BMW, Ben realized why Erin hadn't intercepted him on foot. He watched her black Gestapo car pull around the P3 ramp.

"Would it be weird if I sat in the back seat?"

"Yes. Yes, it would. That would be really weird."

"Then I assume lying down on your back seat would also be weird."

"Yes. Yes, it would, but go ahead and do it anyway."

Maria started driving toward the exit ramp. Erin was driving toward Maria's car. Erin stopped and rolled down her window like she wanted to chat. Maria didn't slow down. She just looked at Erin and did her fingers-waggling wave again.

Once they were on Sixth Avenue, Maria got her pipe out of the ashtray. It had a sticky green bud with crystals and orange hair all over it.

"It's all clear if you want to sit up front."

Ben climbed over the seat at the Sixth and Cherry stoplight.

"You want to get baked? Don't look at me all judgmental. I

only get baked so I can get through the workday."

"No judgment from me, but you're not at work."

"I plan to work on a motion tonight, so technically my workday is still going."

"You want to go get a Rainier at Linda's Tavern instead?"

"Yes. Yes, I would. I could do a Rainier."

Chapter 16

Up at Linda's, instead of a Rainier, they had a few pitchers of Rainier. They smoked a few more bowls too. It wasn't late, but Ben figured heading down to his parents' place that night wasn't going to happen. Ben was pretty wasted. He'd drank more than Maria. Maria was pretty tipsy but more or less in good shape, considering.

"White boy. You want me to take you back to your car?"

"Yeah, I guess."

Ben stumbled out of Linda's. Maria walked, mostly. Maria drove him down to the SMT parking garage. It was only about a three-minute drive. As they pulled into P2, Ben almost expected to see Erin's Mercedes sitting there. It wasn't. He saw the Barracuda sitting alone, the last kid at school, stuck in detention. Ben knew how his car felt. "Yeah, I been there, done that."

"Are you good to drive, white boy?"

"Probably."

"You need a bump?"

She pulled out a little brown-glass coke vial. She unscrewed the top. The lid had a teeny-tiny spoon attached to it.

"Don't look at me all judgmental. I only take a little bump when I'm too drunk to drive home."

"Bring it on."

She scooped up a heaping spoonful, but considering how small the spoon was, it was still barely anything.

"One for the left nostril."

She scooped up a second spoonful.

"And one for the right. That'll get you back to Capitol Hill."

Ben did get back to the neighborhood in one piece, but when he got to his apartment building, he saw Erin's Mercedes. She wasn't in it, but there it was. She wasn't waiting by the front door or over at the teriyaki place around the corner. He was pretty wasted still, and it took a couple of minutes of fiddling before he could get his copied service-entrance key into the lock. "The fuckin' lock kept floating around. And when it would finally stop floating, the key would start floating around. It was like docking two ships moving around each other in outer space." Once he got in, he peeked into the elevator lobby. He didn't want to take the stairs, and he figured if Erin wasn't in the lobby, he was probably good to take the elevator.

The elevator dinged and the door opened. He forgot where he was right at that moment. To Ben, it felt as if he were missing a chunk of time, as he couldn't remember what had happened since he walked by the teriyaki place on Broadway. He quickly gathered that he was in his apartment building, in the elevator, and it had just opened onto his floor. His apartment was around the corner from the elevator bank. He started walking but stopped suddenly. He heard a voice, a conversation, or one side of a phone conversation. He didn't know what it was about, or who the person on the other end of the phone was, but he knew the voice of the person in the hall.

Somehow or other, Erin had managed to get into his building. "Seriously, though, how hard could it be for a pretty blond girl to get someone to let her into an apartment lobby on a cold fall evening?" Ben peeked around the corner and could see her standing near the hall fire escape window by his apartment door. He'd made sure to never let Erin get a copy of his apartment key, and now that foresight had paid off. It took a minute to remember why he was being so cloak and dagger about coming home. But once her saw her, he knew. Luckily her back was turned to him. She should have heard the elevator ding, he thought. Apparently, she didn't. He didn't take the elevator back down. "She didn't hear it ding that first time, but she would probably hear it when the doors opened again." Ben beat a hasty retreat to the stairway door.

Down at the Barracuda, he experienced the floating lock and key syndrome again. It took a minute or two, but he finally managed to get into his car. Weeks later, Ben would wonder how all those little telltale scratches around the driver's side door lock got there. The ignition was a little easier to peg. They aren't flush with the surface like a door lock, and the raised part is like a little cradle to help you get the key in. Ben figured they must make the ignition like that so you can get your car started when you're drunk. It appeared, he thought, to be modeled after a cock and pussy. "It's considerate, because if it's cold outside you can get your car started and get the heat going. A drunk person could freeze in the winter if they couldn't get their car started." Considering how easy they'd made it to start the car, he wondered why they'd made the car's door locks so hard to operate when you're drunk.

Ben was mostly satisfied with that as an explanation. He was still dissatisfied with the car door lock but appreciated the ignition. Then his car door lock made him remember trying to get into his apartment building that night, and he was immediately disappointed by the makers of residential door locks. "It's like they don't even care if drunks freeze to death on their own doorsteps, within a few feet of a warm bed. It's very disappointing to me."

It was cold that night before Thanksgiving, unusually so. It was rarely too cold in Seattle, but that night it was. Ben tried to fall asleep in the back seat of the Barracuda, but he couldn't. After about an hour, he climbed into the driver's seat. He was still seeing double, and the coke had long since worn off, but he figured he had one other option. From where he was sitting, his double vision caused him to see two of Erin's Mercedes. Going to his place was off the table. Going to his parents' house was too far even for him to risk in his state. But Maria had told him over Rainiers at Linda's that she lived at the Gayle.

Ben knew where it was because he'd been there before. His brother's best friend Jack had lived there for a while. It was a year or two after Mike died. Ben had caught the bus to Seattle to go skate up on Capitol Hill. He was by himself. He used to skate all day long on Saturdays and Sundays by himself. That morning, he couldn't sleep. He tried to sleep in, but by ten o'clock he'd given up and rolled out of bed. He ate some raisin bran, packed a peanut butter and jelly sandwich into his backpack, and headed out to catch the bus to downtown Seattle.

"That major-label Jawbreaker record had just come out. The one that Maria was listening to that day in the parking garage. So that was like nineteen ninety-five, then? Yeah, something like that, because I was fourteen. I was listening to it when I was walking by the WaMu bank branch there. All the cool kids who were older than me hated it. 'They sold out' is all I heard that whole summer. Fuck those cool kids anyway. Yeah,

Jawbreaker fuckin' sold out. Who cares. That record was great. It's like you can only be punk if you wash dishes in some greasy spoon during the day and then entertain the scene's elite by playing music for them at night. Because God forbid anyone is ever able to support themselves by doing the very thing that everyone loves them for. Anyway, I saw Jack working at the Vivace on Broadway."

Jack was getting off work, or maybe he just took off after his break or perhaps even spontaneously quit, Ben wasn't quite sure. What Ben was quite sure about was that when he got up to take a piss at Jack's apartment at the Gayle, Jack swiped the Walkman with that Jawbreaker *Dear You* cassette in it out of Ben's backpack. "Jack was like, 'Hey, man, I got to go meet someone. Tell your parents I said hey.'" Ben didn't really care. To be honest, Ben was surprised Jack didn't fully rob him. Based on the place where Mike had been living when he died, Ben had expected Jack to bring him to a similar crack den. He hadn't, though. The building was actually nice. He could tell that Jack was in pretty bad shape. Ben couldn't figure out how Jack had managed to rent the place at all.

Ben never saw Jack after that. He wanted to believe that Jack was alive, but the fact that he never saw him around made Ben think otherwise. The fact that nobody had ever called to let him know where Jack's funeral would be, gave Ben some hope that Jack was alive. As far as the Walkman goes, "People got to do what they got to do to get by. I didn't really give a shit about the Walkman. I hope he sold it for a fix or whatever he needed that day. I was pretty sore about the Jawbreaker cassette, but I got a new copy a couple of months later. Hey, Jack, if you've still got that cassette, go ahead and keep it. If you're still kicking around the planet somewhere, give me a call."

The Gayle was the destination. It was only a few blocks away, and Maria lived there. Ben closed his left eye to make the double vision stop and put the Barracuda in reverse without looking behind him. He backed into three newspaper boxes, toppling them over and sending them skidding a few feet down the sidewalk. He got out to have a look. The *Seattle Times*, *Seattle Weekly*, and the *Stranger*. "Bastards." Ben stood there, inspecting the damage to his bumper. He took a *Stranger* and a *Seattle Weekly*. They were free. He tugged on the *Seattle Times* box, but it was locked. They charged for the *Seattle Times*, and the impact had not popped the little lock that kept the box closed. Ben took his newspapers, got in the Barracuda, closed his left eye, and roared off toward the Gayle.

Chapter 17

Luckily for Jack, the Gayle was only a short ride from his apartment building. Luckily for Jack, Maria's buzzer both worked and was clearly marked with her name. Luckily for Jack, Maria took in strays.

Jack hit the buzzer.

"What?" was her response.

"Is there any way I could sleep on your couch?"

"White boy?"

"Uh-huh."

"Seriously? Is she at your apartment too?"

"I mean . . ."

The telltale click-clack of the secure door unlocking interrupted what was sure to be haphazardly prepared response by Ben. The speaker popped back on.

"Number 102. Don't try no BS up in here. You sleep on the couch, that's it."

"For sure." The fact that he was talking into the speaker now without hitting the call button didn't occur to him until it did.

"Oh, yeah, the fuckin' button thing . . . so I'm just talking to dead air. And now I'm doing it even more. And now I'm just one of those people who roam around Capitol Hill and talk to themselves. Okay, now I'm going to stop talking out loud and

112

go back to just thinking shit instead of saying it."

The click-clack of the door stopped, but Ben had been too involved with his one-sided conversation with himself to grab the door handle and open it. He hit the call button again.

"So, like, I just didn't get the thing in time or whatever."

Maria's voice, distorted by the cheap little door speaker, replied.

"Oh my God, you really are just a helpless little man-baby, aren't you."

"I mean . . ."

"That wasn't a question. You better get the door this time, or you're sleeping in your car, buddy."

Click-clack, click-clack, then the door the buzzer sounded.

"I got you now, fucker."

Ben talking out loud to no one again. That time he did get the door open before the click-clack and buzzing stopped. He was very proud of himself, too proud considering what a simple task pulling on a door was.

Ben began walking through the lobby, where those wall-mounted little mailboxes were. All at once he realized that he had no idea which apartment he was supposed to be going to. It had been easy to locate on the speaker box because her name was next to the call button. He couldn't remember if the call buttons had apartment numbers next to the names, but he didn't want to go back to the secure door. He had a genuine fear that if he went back and held the door open while getting a look at the call box, he'd be locked out and really have to sleep in his car. His next best idea was to try to peek through the door's windowpane and read the apartment numbers off the call box without actually opening the door. "Did she say what apartment she lived in? I'm so fucked up that I honestly don't remember."

After that night, and for the rest of the time Maria lived in that building, Ben never trusted that secure door. He never once walked up to it without his heart skipping a beat, and he never heard it slam behind him without him believing it had just locked him out on the front stoop in the cold. The door had traumatized him into future obedience the way a child is conditioned not to touch a hot stove.

That night, Ben's bewilderment continued for two or three minutes. It was late enough that he would feel bad just knocking on random people's doors, but he was beginning to think that was the only way he'd ever determine which unit Maria lived in. He didn't even know if she was on the first floor or some higher floor. He had walked all the way down the first-floor hall, past each and every anonymous apartment door. The only door left was adorned with one of those bright green exit signs above it. Ben didn't know which door to knock on, but he was pretty sure that the exit door wasn't the way to go.

Nevertheless, he stood and looked at that exit door for another thirty or forty seconds. It was a good focal point in what had become a sea of uncertainty. He didn't want to go out the exit door, but he knew he could. Unlike the anonymous apartment doors, the exit door was one he could open and go through without knocking. He wouldn't have to wake anybody up to go through it. He even found himself speculating that there might be a cozy little stairway on the other side where he could sleep. Turning around to face the secure front door again seemed unthinkable. That hallway was a gauntlet of club-wielding anonymous apartment doors, but the secure front door was the terrifying brick both at the head and at the end of that gauntlet.

For a few seconds, Ben considered just staying where he was. Standing there, his nose no more than three inches from the hundred-year-old lead paint on that exit door, wasn't scary at all. It made sense. If he never moved, he'd never have to be scared of Maria's apartment building. If Ben's knees hadn't hurt so badly, he could have stayed like that for an hour or two. But they did, and he couldn't.

So he turned around. Up until that moment, all the things that had scared him that evening—Erin's Terminator-like persistence and Maria's apartment building—all of a sudden became less scary. Now it was the thing at the end of the hall that was the scariest of all. Maria Deloera, ready for bed in an oversized T-shirt, was terrifying because she made him feel an emotion that he never allowed himself to indulge in: desire.

Chapter 18

Maria stood in her hallway, annoyed. This guy, she thought, needed me to rescue him from having to see his girlfriend, some defense attorney, no less. Then he comes here and asks me if he can stay over. Now he's just staring blankly at the door to the back stairway. She wanted to yell "Oi, dipshit, what the fuck are you doing?" Instead, she just watched him, wondering how long he was going to stare like that. After a minute, she was so fascinated by what was happening, she wasn't even annoyed anymore.

He was just standing there, motionless. She thought he looked like a robot that someone had switched off and pushed into a corner. Maria didn't know if he was lost or was just trying to decide if he should leave. Either was fine with her. She thought he was cute, but nothing was going to happen. Nothing. If he was there because he thought something was going to happen, he really should just go. Seriously, she thought, if she'd wanted something to happen, she would have put on something better than her ex-boyfriend's stretched-out Black Flag T-shirt. She continued to watch him, and then he suddenly turned around. He stood there staring for a few beats before he spoke.

"Oh, your place is back that way."

"Yeah. It's the first apartment on the right when you walk through the front door, number 102. You didn't see the unit number on the call box? And I told you which apartment."

"I was scared of the click-clack and buzzing, so I didn't go back over there."

"What? Did you go back to Linda's and buy acid from that guy who hangs out in the corner booth?"

"Um, I don't know what we're talking about any more."

"Me either. Do you want to sleep?"

"Yeah."

"Come on."

Maria's couch was comfy. She brought out a fuzzy blanket and squishy pillow. The pillow was too squishy, and Ben put his head down on one of the firmer couch pillows instead. The squishy pillow seemed like the sort of pillow a girl might put between her legs when she was sleeping. After Maria went into the bathroom, Ben immediately buried his face in it to see if he could catch a whiff of her pussy on it. When she came out of the bathroom, she gave him a cheap toothbrush still in its packaging. "Don't use my toothbrush! Use this."

Ben took the new toothbrush into Maria's bathroom. He unwrapped it, put some toothpaste on it, and ran it under the faucet. He didn't feel like brushing his teeth, but he did suck on Maria's toothbrush while he was pissing. He wanted to see how her mouth tasted. When he first entered the bathroom, he looked for a hamper. He was actually glad he didn't find one because he would have started playing with her dirty underwear immediately. There was no lock on her bathroom, and he imagined that her walking in while he had four or five of her thongs laid out on the bath mat could get weird.

When he came out of the bathroom, Maria was already in

bed. Her bedroom light was out, and she told him to turn out the living room light and go to sleep. So that's what he did.

Chapter 19

Ben didn't sleep through the night. Nobody sleeps through the night. At least, Ben had never known anyone who slept through the night. Ben woke up every couple of hours. He never really had to pee, but since he was awake, he always got up and went anyway. When he woke up, his throat was always dry, so he'd get a drink from the bathroom faucet. He heard Maria get up once and use the bathroom too. Then she went right back to her bedroom and was quiet again. He was up around seven, the third time since he'd fallen asleep. Daylight was just starting to creep into the apartment, but just a little. After all, this was still Seattle, and even plain old morning daylight is mostly cloaked by an unending blanket of clouds. He was definitely a little hung over, so he dozed off again.

He woke up again around nine. Maria was up. The stretched-out T-shirt and bare legs had been replaced by a black spaghetti-strap top and faded Levis. She had on some sort of designer black boots, the kind with wedged heels.

"You awake, white boy? You want to get some coffee?"

"Yeah, all right."

"Where you going today? What did you say yesterday, your parents' house?

"Yeah, my parents' place in Tacoma. You?"

"The original plan was to leave last night after work and drive home to Yakima, but Snoqualmie Pass was pretty bad last night. I thought it might be a little better this morning, but it still looks pretty snowed in from the weather reports."

"What else goes out there? White Pass?"

"Oh, you'd like it if I had to take White Pass, wouldn't you, white boy. How come it's White Pass anyway? Why can't it be Brown Pass, or better yet Latina Pass? There are certainly enough of us on the other side of the mountains to warrant naming a couple of things after us."

This was exactly the sort of question Ben was uncomfortable answering. After all, despite being born in Seattle, he was acutely aware that he was essentially squatting on ill-gotten land. Naming the city after the chief of the Duwamish and Suquamish always seemed more like a slap in the face to Native Americans from his ancestors than an accolade. He started to speak what would certainly be a jumbled mess of a response, but all that came out was "Um."

Maria was just fucking with him, and when she saw Ben trying to formulate a politically correct response in his culturally ignorant little brain, she stepped in and saved him from saying something stupid.

"But no, seriously, White Pass isn't any better. Even if they say it's passable with chains, that just means that you're going to be stuck in the middle of the pass in a five-mile-long line of cars sitting in one place for seven or eight hours. I actually spent a whole Christmas day sitting in my car on White Pass a couple of years ago. The risk of getting stuck in the mountains in your car just isn't worth it."

"Come to Tacoma with me."

"Thanksgiving with the white boy's family?"

"You're from eastern Washington. You can watch the Apple Cup with my dad."

"Hey, smart guy, the Apple Cup is next Saturday, not today."

"Whatever. What the fuck do I know about football? I fuckin' hate football. But my dad loves it. There're always football games on when I go down there on Thanksgiving. So watch some other game with him."

"And what do you do while the football game is on?'

"I just hang around in the kitchen and do shots of Jameson with my mom. And I eat a bunch of the food while she's still getting it ready. Then I feel bad that nobody is helping her, so I volunteer to help, and then she kicks me out of the kitchen for eating all the stuffing while I'm fluffing it. You'll have a good time. I promise."

"Does your dad have any beer?"

"He's got a refrigerator full of Rainier, just like I do at my place."

"Calm down, white boy. We're not going to your place."

"Yeah, not today, but probably some other time."

"Sure we are," she said with obvious sarcasm. "All right, we're off to North Tacoma."

"Sorry, but we're going to South Tacoma."

"Ew, seriously? That's too bad. I've heard North Tacoma is nice. All right, let's go before I change my mind. We have to go get a latte at Vivace first."

"For sure."

Maria and Ben walked out to the Barracuda. Ben walked around back to see the damage the newspaper boxes had done to his bumper. He wasn't happy with what he saw, but he had braced himself for much worse. The Barracuda was old, so it had a chrome-steel bumper, not like newer cars, where the bumper is painted and effectively just part of the frame. The Barracuda's bumper was definitely tweaked from the newspaper box collision the night before, but it wasn't tragic. Ben figured nobody would even really notice it. Right then, Maria walked around the rear of the car on her way to the passenger side.

"Wow, what happened to your bumper? That's super fucked up. Too bad. It's a great car otherwise."

"Yeah. You know, I cannot stand those fuckheads at the *Seattle Times*, the *Stranger*, and *Seattle Weekly*.

"What?"

"Nothing. I just got a score to settle with those fuckers."

"All right. Let's get some coffee, seriously."

Tacoma's city flag should be a graffitied Abrams tank shooting an Olde English 800 forty-ounce bottle at an old brick factory's smokestack. In reality, the actual Tacoma flag was warm and a little disarming. Maybe that was the point: to charmingly disarm people casually passing through the city so that the locals can shanghai and rob them.

South Tacoma was the most Tacoma part of Tacoma. It was the crossroads of the city. In equal parts, the violent gang war of the eastside spilled into a south end that was still partially engulfed by the remnants of the Hilltop neighborhood's 1980s crack epidemic and abutted a west end that fancied itself too fancy for the rest of Tacoma. The only parts of the city that South Tacoma didn't touch was North Tacoma and Northeast Tacoma. North Tacoma was where the bourgie fuckers were, so fuck them anyway. Northeast Tacoma was all the way on the other side of the tide flats. So seriously, that isn't even really Tacoma at all. It was sort of how West Seattle wasn't really

Seattle, just that place on the other side of the port.

Driving through South Tacoma, Pacific Avenue divided the Puyallup reservation and the Latino part of town on the east from the Korean part of town on the west. As you continued south, various Korean neighborhoods faded into various Black neighborhoods and eventually became poor white neighborhoods. Those poor neighborhoods near the south corner, the places where GIs from JBLM who didn't want to live on base or in Lakewood settled, that was where Ben called home.

By noon it was raining. It was always raining, especially between October and May. "Jack and Mike always called those months the dark wet." By Thanksgiving 2010, the dark wet was in full swing.

The Northwest was generally gray and wet most of the year in most places. Tacoma, and more specifically South Tacoma, was grayer and wetter than everywhere else in the Northwest, at least it seemed so to Ben. "It was accurate to say a dark cloud hung over the Pacific Northwest, and an even darker cloud hung over my house."

Maria and Ben pulled up to Ben's parents' house, which was painted gray. The loose pebbles that peeled off the city's cheap gravel-over-tar street were gray. The neighbor's chain-link fence was gray. Even the grass in front of his parents' house appeared to be gray. Big Ben, Ben's mom Barbara, and his little sister Lisa came out to the front porch when they heard Ben's car pull up. Ben wondered if his family was ill, because they all looked somehow gray. Ben's eyes drifted from his family, across the lawn, and to the dirt where a sidewalk should be. Apparently, the city had determined that this street didn't warrant a luxury accommodation like a sidewalk, but if it had, that sidewalk would have been gray.

Even after several years, Maria still wasn't completely accustomed to western Washington. East of the mountains, there was life: flowers and orchards and fields of grass alive with vibrant colors.

She said, "Am I wearing monochrome glasses? How come there are no flowers here? You know all those depressing muted filters you can use on photos now? I'm beginning to think western Washington is where those came from. Every day around here just seems like a slight variation on some drab gray photo filter. Light gray is November. Gray is December. Dark gray is January. Darker gray is February, brownish gray is March. Et cetera. Et cetera. Et cetera."

"What about the spring and summer months?"

"What did I just say white boy? Et cetera. Et cetera. Et cetera. I'm surprised you aren't gray, but then again, your tone of white could be a washed-out gray. It really never is the right color around here. I never really put my finger on it until we turned down this street."

Maria stepped out of the Barracuda and somehow immediately splashed her own vibrant color all over the canvas of that Thanksgiving. Ben was only half joking about Maria watching football with Big Ben, but she really did sit in the living room for two hours watching football with him. The two of them drank so many Rainiers that Ben had to go down to the ampm to get another half rack. The ampm was right down the road, but driving there was still pretty sketchy, since he'd been pounding shots of Jameson with his little sister and mom in the kitchen.

After dinner, Big Ben took Ben and Maria to the garage to show them the 1968 Mustang Fastback he was restoring. The 390-ci V8 was sitting on a work bench next to the cherry picker

Big Ben had used to hoist it out of the engine compartment. The freshly rebuilt motor had the chrome Edelbrock valve covers and air cleaner. There were new five-spoke Crager rims and BFGoodrich radials. There was sanded Bondo where Big Ben had done his own bodywork and gray primer all over the body of that Mustang.

Big Ben said, "The motor's ready to go back in. I can't do the paint job myself, but I got a buddy at Sauro's Body Shop who is going to do a high-end black with white racing stripes. How's the Barracuda holding up?"

"Pretty good. I tweaked the bumper a little the other day."

"Pull it around to the garage. If it's just a little bent, I can pop that back into shape."

Maria went back into the house. It was almost time for pumpkin pie, and Ben's mom roped Maria into doing a couple more shots of Jameson with her.

It had been at least six months since Ben had been home. Lisa was already sixteen. It seemed like every time he saw her, she was a different person. Not really a different person, but people change so much at that age, if you don't see them every day it seems like they've morphed into an adult overnight. She looked like an adult woman—a young woman, but still mostly like an adult. People that age often look like adults, but a brief conversation is all that's needed to uncover that you are indeed speaking to a child. It even happened at work. The Rule 9 interns were actually adults, but they were mostly still in their early twenties. Ben was turning twenty-nine in a couple of weeks, and it always blew him away at how different a person he already was from these interns, who were only a few years younger than he was. Lisa was old enough to drive. Soon she'd be old enough to go to college and buy beer.

At sixteen, she was apparently old enough to get stoned, because she grabbed Ben and Maria and took them out to the side of the house and got them baked. The age of strong weed was upon Washington State. In not much more than a year, it would be legal. The potency of what Lisa had was nothing like anything Ben had smoked before. Afterward, Ben went up to his old room and fell asleep for an hour while Barbara, Lisa, and Big Ben entertained Maria. Fortunately, or unfortunately for her, the way Ben's family entertained typically involved more shots of Jameson. Since it was Thanksgiving, everyone also ate more pumpkin pie and ice cream.

Ben could have slept another hour or two, but he woke up to the sound of retching coming from the upstairs bathroom next to Ben's and Lisa's bedrooms. When he knocked, he was surprised to hear Maria respond.

"I'm okay. I'll be out in a minute."

She thought it was Lisa or Barbara checking on her.

"It's Ben. Are you really okay?"

Maria opened the bathroom door. She was sitting on the floor.

"Your family is out of control."

"Outta control, no way. They're fuckin' boiler plate for around here, garden variety white trash."

"They sure know how to entertain company."

"I said you'd have fun, didn't I?"

"Yep, good time."

Maria put her hand out.

"Help me up. These jeans are too tight now. I ate too much."

"Ate?"

"Ate too much, drank too much, smoked too much. Where did your sister get that weed?"

Ben pulled Maria up to her feet. They were face to face, only an inch or two apart.

"What happens now?" Maria said.

"Behind you. That green toothbrush, it's mine. You can use it."

"Ha ha, because of last night."

"Yeah, that, but seriously, you should brush your teeth."

"Yeah, I'm going to do that right now."

Oddly enough, nothing was embarrassing or weird for either of them. Maria just spun around, turned on the faucet, puked a bit in the sink, and picked up Ben's toothbrush. She started brushing with the sort of vigor you'd expect from someone with a mouthful of regurgitated whiskey and pumpkin pie. Ben let her finish before he reminded her that the toothpaste was in the medicine cabinet. Maria smacked herself on the forehead with her open palm like she was some sort of slapstick vaudeville drunkard. Then she brushed for real.

They walked downstairs together. Ben had his arm around her shoulder, more to steady Maria than anything, but his family took this as an overt show of mutual affection. Ben had never said he was with Maria. Maria had never said they were a couple. But neither of them had ever said they weren't together.

Barbara was pretty sloshed herself. She started gushing, "You two are so goddamn adorable. Let me get a picture. Hang on, hang on, hang on."

It took Barbara at least five minutes to find her camera in the hall closet. It took five more for her to figure out if there was film in it. She ultimately got her picture, but she was so wasted that she snapped it crooked and off-center. To this day, that trainwreck of a photo resides in one of Barbara's family photo albums.

Ben loaded Maria into the passenger side of the Barracuda like a sack of groceries. Ben never wore a seat belt, but he strapped Maria into hers just the same. He yanked the shoulder harness extra tight on her. It was still raining, but it was just that late evening sprinkling that happened every night around bedtime, not the ice-cold darts of marble-sized water that fell before dinnertime. All in all, the drive back to Seattle was uneventful. Maria was out cold in the passenger's seat by the time they crossed into King County. She stayed that way until Ben pulled up to the Gayle to drop her off.

He nudged her.

"You're home."

The way she'd passed out, she was lurched forward but being held up by the extra-snug seat belt. It was, in a word, hilarious.

"Maria, you gotta get up. We're at your place."

Nothing.

He turned on that Jawbreaker CD, the major label one.

Nothing.

He turned it up louder, and Maria gasped herself awake.

"You're home."

She looked at him. She didn't say anything. For a minute, Ben wondered if she was just too wasted to talk. She had that blank stare that intoxicated people get.

He didn't say anything.

Then she leaned in, either because she was falling toward him or because she was trying to kiss him. He couldn't tell which. Either way, Ben had snugged the seat belt up so much when he loaded her into the car that she was effectively pinned to the back of the seat.

The Barracuda had leather bucket seats, so Ben couldn't scoot over to the passenger's side where Maria was sitting. Instead, he clicked the button on the seat-belt harness, causing her to fall across the center console and into him. He pulled her in closer and reached out with his left hand and put it on her right thigh.

"Aren't you going out with Erin O'Connell?"

"Sort of. Maybe. Does it matter?"

Ben kissed her.

"Did you really pee on Tim's shoes?"

"Does that seem like something that I, a respectable licensed attorney, a prosecutor for the city of Seattle would do?"

Lawyers always answer questions with questions.

"So that's a yes?"

It had been bugging Ben since his first day at the city attorney's office. He knew he'd seen Maria before.

"Didn't you used to be in a hardcore band?"

"Does being in a hardcore band seem like something that I, a respectable licensed attorney, a prosecutor for the city of Seattle would do?"

She kissed him and then abruptly stopped. Maria got out of the Barracuda and started toward her building's stoop. Ben pushed in the clutch, ready to put the Barracuda into first gear. Maria turned around, bent over, and leaned into the Barracuda through the rolled-down passenger-side window.

"You coming in or what?"

About the Author

I was a homeless teenager. Now I own a home. I was a high school dropout. Now I'm an attorney. I was an alcoholic. Now I'm sober. I was a kid well into adulthood. Now I'm the adult parent of kids. I was alone. Now I have people. I was a punk rock teenager. Now I'm a punk rock middleager . I was a talker. Now I'm a writer.

Thanks for reading. I'll see you back for Book Two. Please follow and leave review at any or all of the links below.

You can connect with me on:

🌐 https://blandcoffeepublishing.com

📘 https://www.facebook.com/ christopher.stockwell.5

🔗 https://blandcoffeepublishing.com

🔗 https://www.bookbub.com/ profile/christopher-j-stockwell

🔗 https://www.goodreads.com/ author/show/39540330.
Christopher_J_Stockwell

🔗 https://www.amazon.com/ stores/Christopher-J.-Stockwell/
author/B0C738J98J? ref=ap_rdr&isDramIntegrated=true&
shoppingPortalEnabled=true

🔗 https://www.linkedin.com/ company/bland-coffee-
publishing-llc/?viewAsMember=true

Also by Christopher J. Stockwell

Sleeping in the Daytime
Look through drunken and fatigued eyes at a Pacific Northwest that no longer exists. Charming loser Jack will be your tour guide to places on the underside of society few dare to tread.

Courting Mediocrity
A quiet life, in a quiet town, with a sweet girl just isn't Jack's style. There are still so many bridges to burn and allies to alienate. The guardrails are gone, and Jack is passed out at the wheel.

Squatting in the Shadow of an Ant
The good will and patience of others goes only so far. What happens to a lovable fuck up when everyone else had moved on with their life. They end up somewhere, but where?

The Complete Down and Out in Seattle and Tacoma Series

The three novellas of the Down and Out in Seattle and Tacoma Series were written as, and intended to be, just one novel. Buy the entire series together in paperback or limited edition hardcover.

The Antagonist's Handbook

A pair of losers from the PNW start out for stardom by moving to Los Angeles. After becoming paparazzi, they soon figure out that they can blackmail celebrities into posing for their photos. Eventually, they launch their own tabloid. This is out of print.

I don't even have a copy, and I can't find the contract with the publishing house, so I don't know if I own the rights. That's what happens when you drink too much whiskey and snort too much coke. If you find a copy, let me know. I'll buy it off you.

City Attorney's Office Book Two: The Land of Lollipops and Suckers
Now that Ben understands how to wield the power of the prosecutor's office, how will he use it. He's always wanted for someone to let him inside the machine so he can mess around with the gears and pulleys.

Will that government machine make him a good little cog, or will he throw ideological money wrenches into it. We sort of already know the answer, but watching how he gets there is usually entertaining.

www.ingramcontent.com/pod-product-compliance
Lightning Source LLC
Chambersburg PA
CBHW030004010826
48973CB00009B/2663